P9-BZN-039

THOMAS PAINE

CRUSADER
for
LIBERTY

Also by Albert Marrin

A Volcano Beneath the Snow: John Brown's War Against Slavery
Black Gold: The Story of Oil in Our Lives
Flesh and Blood So Cheap: The Triangle Fire and Its Legacy

National Book Award Finalist
ALBERT MARRIN

THOMAS PAINE

CRUSADER
for
LIBERTY

How one man's ideas
helped form a new nation

ALFRED A. KNOPF
NEW YORK

THIS IS A BORZOI BOOK PUBLISHED BY ALFRED A. KNOPF

Text copyright © 2014 by Albert Marrin
Jacket art and interior illustrations of flag and quill copyright © 2014 by Shutterstock
Jacket illustration of Thomas Paine copyright © 2014 by the Library of Congress

All rights reserved. Published in the United States by Alfred A. Knopf, an imprint of Random House Children's Books,
a division of Random House LLC, a Penguin Random House Company, New York.

Knopf, Borzoi Books, and the colophon are registered trademarks of Random House LLC.

For image credits, please see page 153.

Visit us on the Web! randomhouse.com/kids

Educators and librarians, for a variety of teaching tools, visit us at RHTeachersLibrarians.com

Library of Congress Cataloging-in-Publication Data
Marrin, Albert.
Thomas Paine : crusader for liberty : how one man's ideas helped form a new nation / Albert Marrin. — First edition.
pages   cm
ISBN 978-0-375-86674-6 (trade) — ISBN 978-0-375-96674-3 (lib. bdg.) — ISBN 978-0-385-38605-0 (ebook)
1. Paine, Thomas, 1737–1809—Juvenile literature. 2. Political scientists—United States—Biography—Juvenile
literature. 3. Revolutionaries—United States—Biography—Juvenile literature. 4. United States—History—Revolution,
1775–1783—Juvenile literature. I. Title.
JC178.V5M43 2014
320.51092—dc23
[B]
2013033272

The text of this book is set in 13-point Galliard.

MANUFACTURED IN CHINA

November 2014

10 9 8 7 6 5 4 3 2 1

First Edition

Random House Children's Books supports the First Amendment and celebrates the right to read.

To the memory of those who stood up in "the times that tried men's souls"

History is not history unless it is the truth.

—Abraham Lincoln

Contents

The Age of Paine

*I know not whether any man in the world has had
more influence on its inhabitants or affairs for
the last thirty years than Tom Paine. . . .
Call it then the Age of Paine.*

—John Adams, October 29, 1805

Thomas Paine always stirred strong feelings in others. As a friend recalled, "He never appears but we love and hate him." A slim, soft-spoken man, around five feet ten inches tall, he was not handsome; many thought him downright ugly. "His manners polite and engaging," Paine had a high forehead, long brown hair tied in a ponytail, and a "blazing-red face dotted with purple blotches." His large red nose nearly covered his upper lip. Children would run after him, bawling:

> *Tom Paine is coming from far, from far;*
> *His nose is like a blazing star!*[1]

1

A pictorial tribute to Thomas Paine, "A Man of Two Worlds" (L'homme de deux mondes). *(c. 1809)*

Paine had a first-rate memory; even in old age he remembered details of long-ago events. "His head," an American admirer noted, "was like an orange—it had a separate apartment for everything it contained." Yet his strongest feature was his blue eyes. Such eyes! People marveled at them. Benjamin Franklin, a good friend, was fascinated by "those wonderful eyes of his." Another man thought the flashing eyes "the eyes of an apostle." Paine's eyes, "full of fire," hinted at the emotions boiling inside him.[2]

An outspoken man, Paine talked endlessly, a critic observed. "Vain beyond all belief," he simply could not see things from another's point of view. Paine thought those who agreed with him wise and virtuous, true lovers of humanity. Since he couldn't believe that opponents could be anything other than fools and villains, insults poured from the tips of his turkey-quill pens. Critics were, to him, "scribbling and witless curs," men of "a bewildered mind," afflicted with the "imbecility of an inferior reptile." Of course, this aspect of his personality made Paine lifelong enemies, embittering him further.[3]

Paine also had a softer side. A humane person, "he was always charitable to the poor beyond his means"; that is, he gave with an open hand though needy himself. During the murderous chaos of the French Revolution, he gave the gift of life, helping fugitives—including a man who had publicly slapped his face—escape the executioner.[4]

In certain ways, Paine will always be a mystery. Much of what we would like to know about him is unknown and unknowable. The public Paine was a celebrity, his name known to millions. Of his private life, however, we have only the slightest hints.

To learn about the past, historians rely upon documents written at the time: official records, diaries, letters, autobiographies, and newspaper accounts. Paine kept his personal papers in a wooden trunk, which the son of a friend took charge of after his death. Sadly, when the barn in which the trunk was stored caught fire, this

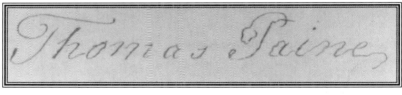

Thomas Paine's signature.

treasure trove went up in smoke. None of Paine's letters remain except the ones kept by their recipients. And unless these people made copies for themselves, we do not know what they wrote to him in return.

We do know that Paine came to America out of desperation, a failure at everything he tried in his native

England. A man of humble background, self-educated through reading, he sought neither wealth nor power. Paine was an intellectual—one who loves ideas and tries to influence the thinking of others. By themselves, ideas are merely thoughts and images we form in our minds. An idea, such as truth or virtue, has no substance or body. You cannot see, hear, touch, taste, or smell it. Nevertheless, ideas are powerful forces that shape not only the individual's approach to life, but society and thus history.

Abraham Lincoln wisely said, "The past is the cause of the present, and the present will be the cause of the future." This is because ideas spoken or put down in writing can set hearts afire. Ideas inspire us to action, sparking change. Every invention and scientific discovery begins in a person's mind, as do acts of decency and charity—and yes, every war and act of bigotry. Similarly, every historical development has roots in an idea, or set of ideas. Yet people, being human, never agree about everything. This may lead to dispute, dispute to quarreling, and quarreling to violence. In short, ideas can kill.

As with any field of knowledge, history has various branches. For example, specialists study the history of politics, economics, and foreign relations. They also study the role of ideas in society. Over time, ideas change to meet new real-world challenges. In this way, "truths" once taken for granted, like "The earth is flat" or "Witches cause lightning storms," give way to newer truths.

Thomas Paine lived during the Enlightenment. Beginning in the late 1600s and lasting until about 1800, this was a time of swift, dramatic change. Rejecting traditional ways of looking at the world, "advanced" thinkers saw human reason as the best, really the *only,* means of finding truth. By relying on experimentation and careful observation to learn about the natural world, they hoped to end ignorance and poverty, war and oppression.

The Enlightenment was also a time of intense conflict. Europeans and Americans began to ask big questions. Is government by kings and nobles right? If not, how should things be changed for the better? Who should do the changing? Should nations have colonies—far-off places where people settle but are still under the rule of the country they came from? If so, how should the mother country treat them? If she treats them unjustly, what can they do about it? Nothing? Beg for reform? Rebel and form nations of their own? What kind of nations? Is democracy good? Should every person—rich

A portrait of Thomas Paine sitting at his desk. (c. 1792–1793)

and poor, male and female, smart and stupid—have an equal voice in governing? Does anybody have the right to enslave another person?

Thomas Paine tackled all these questions. This book, then, is more than a biography. It is about a man's life *and* ideas, and how they influenced the times in which he lived—and continue to wield great influence today. Paine expressed his ideas in scores of essays, including three of the most widely read works of the eighteenth century. In *Common Sense,* he urged Americans to fight for their independence from England. In *Rights of Man,* he defended the French Revolution against critics and proposed a series of social reforms that today we take for granted. In *The Age of Reason,* he attacked organized religion and championed free thought, the right to form one's own religious ideas without fear of sanction.

Writing did not come easily to Thomas Paine. He wrote slowly, slaving over each sentence to express himself clearly. A theme runs through his writings like a golden thread: liberty. "Where liberty is, there is my country," Benjamin Franklin once told him. "Where liberty is not, there is my country," Paine replied. He believed that people are born free. All have the same "natural rights," which can never be taken or given away because they are God-given. Chief among these are the rights to think for oneself, speak freely, and resist oppression.[5]

True to his ideas, Paine took part in revolutions in America and France, and in an almost-revolution in England. In America, he related to the young nation's leaders, including five future presidents: George Washington, John Adams, Thomas Jefferson, James Madison, and James Monroe. He was known as the father of American independence, with Benjamin Franklin telling him, "You, Thomas Paine, are more responsible than any other living person on this continent for the creation of what are called the United States of America."[6]

Paine's zeal for liberty infuriated those fearful of democratic change. In England, the official hangman burned his writings—as if fire could extinguish ideas. In France, the author narrowly escaped beheading during the Reign of Terror. During his last years in America, his criticisms of organized religion made him an outcast, hated and shunned even by former friends. Yet, despite all, Paine's writings became basic texts for champions of liberty on both sides of the Atlantic. They still are.

CHAPTER 1

Portrait of a Failure

Laws grind the poor, and rich men rule the law.
—Oliver Goldsmith, *The Traveller*, 1764

ENGLAND

The future writer and revolutionary was born on January 29, 1737, in a thatched cottage in Thetford, a small town in the English county of Norfolk, some ninety miles northeast of London. Named Thomas, he was the only surviving child of Joseph Pain and his wife, Frances. (In his twenties, Thomas added the *e* to his last name; to avoid confusion, we will always use Paine.) A daughter born the following year soon died, a common tragedy, since half the infants born in Europe died before their second year because of poor diet and disease.

Frances was eleven years older than her husband and nearly forty when she gave birth to Thomas. Neighbors had a low opinion of her. She was, they recalled, "a woman of sour temper," sharp-tongued, petty, and quick to take offense.

The birthplace of Thomas Paine in Thetford, England. (c. 1870–1900)

Most likely, this was due to regrets at having married "beneath her station," that is, lower on the social scale than her own family. One's place in eighteenth-century society depended upon family background, wealth, and religion. The daughter of a successful attorney, Frances belonged to the Church of England, the established, or official, state church. Only its members could sit on the throne, hold public office, or obtain a government job.[1]

Frances's husband was a gentle, easygoing man, a corset maker by trade. To give them narrow waists, fashionable ladies wore linen corsets stiffened with whalebone, laced so tightly that they made breathing hard. A skilled artisan, Joseph carefully sewed the polished strips of whalebone into place. He was also a Quaker, one of several Protestant groups called nonconformists because they did not follow, or conform to, the teachings of the Church of England. Besides Quakers (also known as the Society of Friends), nonconformists included Baptists, Methodists, and Presbyterians. Thomas attended both his parents' places of worship.

Whatever their religion, English people believed their country the most advanced on earth. They took pride in their overseas colonies, in the Royal Navy—the world's largest—and, most of all, in the British constitution. This is not a written document like the United States Constitution, but all the laws and customs relating to the monarch and Parliament, the national legislature. The constitution guaranteed rights unknown anywhere outside England and her American colonies: trial by jury, free speech, and habeas corpus, Latin for "present the body." This meant that a person arrested for a crime must be either formally charged

An illustration from Cassell's History of England *showing King John signing the Magna Carta. (c. 1902)*

and put on trial within a short time or released. Else-where in Europe, the authorities could keep suspects in jail for years without pressing charges or giving them their day in court. France, Spain, Italy, Russia, and some German states allowed torture in order to gain evidence or a confession. Unable to bear the pain, people often confessed to crimes they did not commit.

The British constitution rests on a central principle: nobody is above the law. The idea that there is one law for everyone, no matter their station in life, originated in the Middle Ages. In June 1215, the nobility forced King John, who had ruled pretty much as he liked, to sign the Magna Carta, or Great Charter. His Majesty agreed (Article 39) that "no free person shall be taken or imprisoned or dispossessed, or outlawed, or ban-ished, or in any way destroyed . . . except by the legal judgment of his peers or the law of the land." Kings learned that they broke the law at their peril. For exam-ple, King Charles I was publicly tried and beheaded in 1649, and King James II was driven out of the country for "high crimes and misdemeanors" in 1688.

The rule of law, however, did not mean political, social, or economic equality. Far from it. In young Thomas Paine's day, government was of, by, and for a few thousand wealthy families. The king, nobility, leading landlords, lawyers, merchants, and bankers controlled every aspect of public life. One needed a certain amount of property to vote or run for office. For example, Thetford, a town of two thousand, had only thirty-one qualified voters. This meant that just a tiny minority of men, and no women, had a voice in making the laws. (Women were thought to lack the intelligence to make important decisions.) Wealthy men voted other wealthy men, or their own followers, into Parliament. The king, however, was the wealthiest person in the realm. So His Majesty usually got the laws he wanted by offering members "golden pills," or government posts with grand titles, big salaries, and little if any work to do.

England's wealthy saw themselves as a race apart, naturally superior to everyone else. Inequality, supposedly, was God's law, meant to keep the lowly in their place. As Samuel Johnson, among the greatest English writers of his day, declared: "Mankind are happier in a state of inequality and subordination." The lot of those "common wretches that crawl upon the earth," others said, was "to be born and eat and sleep and die, and be forgotten."[2]

A familiar jingle went:

It is a sin
To steal a pin.

Parents drilled this into their children's heads, for anyone with eyes to see and ears to hear knew that almost any misdeed could cost you your life.[3]

Eighteenth-century England was a place where life was cheap. Savage laws protected property. When Thomas was a boy, some 250 offenses carried the death penalty. These ranged from high treason and murder to burglary, arson, rape, highway robbery, picking pockets, counterfeiting, and fishing or hunting on private estates.

Justice was truly blind, as the law made no distinction between young and old, between serious and petty crimes. Newspapers routinely reported executions that would be unthinkable in any civilized country today. We read, for example, of a boy of ten hanged for steal-

An illustration of Ann Beddingfield being burned at the stake in England for the murder of her husband.
(c. 1763)

ing a penknife. A hungry seven-year-old girl went to the gallows for snatching a petticoat, and a fourteen-year-old girl for taking a handkerchief from a shop. Afterward, an official announcement read: "Let children beware of committing crimes, for their youth will not always save them." All executions were carried out in public, before large audiences, as warnings to would-be offenders.[4]

Until 1789, English women were strangled and their bodies burned at the stake for killing their husbands, even in self-defense. This law, a judge explained, was "founded on a well-known part of the Christian religion which says,

'That wives should be obedient to their husbands in all things.'" Nor could someone charged with "self-murder"—suicide—escape punishment. The *Gentleman's Magazine* described how an angry crowd dug up a suicide's body, "dragged his guts about the highway, poked his eyes out, and broke almost all his bones." Whipping and branding on the cheek with a red-hot iron punished non-death-penalty offenses, such as loitering or begging in forbidden places. If you owed money to a merchant, he could have you put in debtors' prison until a relative or friend paid up. If not, you rotted in a damp, dark, dirty dungeon.[5]

Thomas saw the law's cruelty with his own eyes. His cottage stood alongside the main road, with a clear view of Gallows Hill, a bare chalk ridge used for hangings. The youngster often peered from a window as the condemned shuffled past in chains. Afterward, he watched their bodies outlined against the sky, swinging back and forth in the breeze. They swung for an hour to make sure they were dead and as a lesson to children about the "wages of sin."

GROWING YEARS

When Thomas turned seven, his parents enrolled him in the Thetford Grammar School. Though it cost little, they had to scrimp and save to afford the fees. Yet Joseph would not allow his son to learn Latin, required for studies like medicine and law. Quakers believed England's ruling classes used the language of the ancient Romans to instill obedience and thus keep power in their own hands. Instead of Latin, Thomas took "practical" subjects like reading, writing, arithmetic, and bookkeeping. The headmaster thought him "a sharp boy, of unsettled application," that is, smart but lazy. Anyhow, his parents took him out of school after five years, at the age of twelve. From then on, he would educate himself through reading and in the school of hard knocks, or real-life experiences.[6]

Joseph took his son into his shop to learn corset making. Though a fast learner, Thomas grew

The Thetford Grammar School, which Thomas Paine attended as a boy. Though larger now, at the time Paine attended, this building made up the entire school. (c. 2011)

restless by his late teens. Bursting with youthful energy and a thirst for adventure, he wanted to see the world beyond Thetford. His chance came just as he turned nineteen.

England and France were again at war. Known as the Seven Years' War (1756–1763) in Europe, and the French and Indian War in North America, it was a struggle over trade and colonies. Above all, England wanted to drive the French from Canada, where they had threatened the security of its thirteen American colonies

THE *Privateer Ship*
Duke of Cumberland,
Capt. JAMES LILLY,
Mounting 16 SIX-POUNDERS, and is to carry 120 Men : Is now lying at the Watering-Place, and will proceed on her intended Cruize in a Week from the Date hereof : She is a compleat Ship and a prime failer. All Gentlemen Seamen and others, who intend making a Cruize, are defired to repair on board.

NOTICE IS HEREBY GIVEN,

THAT no Non-Subfcriber will for the future be admitted to the Dancing-Affembly, unlefs a Ticket be obtained from one of the Directors for his Admiffion, for which Application muft be made, at their Houfes, before

Privateer advertisement from the *New York Mercury*,
December 4, 1758, during the Seven Years War.
(Courtesy of the Collection of The New-York Historical Society)

An ad in the New York Mercury *seeking men to work aboard a privateer.*

for more than a century. Joined by Indian tribes, such as the Huron and the Ottawa, French troops raided along the frontier from the Great Lakes to Virginia. Wherever the raiders struck, they left burned settlements and murdered farm families.

One day, Thomas saw a newspaper ad for bold lads to sail aboard the privateer *Terrible* under Captain William Death. Privateers were not pirate ships manned by outlaws, but privately owned vessels operating under official licenses. Governments used them as an inexpensive way of attacking enemy trade, freeing their navies to strike at warships. When a privateer captured a merchant ship, called a prize, the owners sold it and its cargo, giving each crew member a share of the profits.

Thomas ran away to London, the nation's capital, and signed on to the *Terrible*. Joseph, however, feared for his son's life and, worse, for his morals. He knew that privateering was unusually dangerous and that ships were generally crewed by "broken-down men"— thieves, gamblers, and fugitives from the law. So he followed Thomas to London and talked him into staying ashore. A lucky thing, too, for the *Terrible* had a terrible voyage. In the English Channel, she met a French privateer. After a ferocious cannon duel, 150 crew members, including Captain Death, lay dead. Only seventeen survived, most with dreadful wounds.

Rather than return to Thetford, Thomas decided to work for a London corset maker. The capital was a dazzling place, a different world from rural Thetford. With a population of over six hundred thousand, the city was the largest on earth.

For the wealthy, London was a paradise of elegance and culture. Stately mansions, modeled on royal palaces, stood amid private parks surrounded by iron-rail fences. Each mansion had scores of servants: cooks, maids, gardeners, coachmen, and butlers. Dark-skinned Africans, usually former slaves, were especially desirable as servants because they seemed so exotic in an otherwise all-white society. Family portraits often depicted blacks wearing colorful velvet costumes, silver-buckled shoes, and powdered wigs.

For the poor—the vast majority—London was a nightmare of teeming slums, vile smells, and open sewers running beside cobblestone streets. "Nothing in London makes a more detestable sight than the butchers' stall," wrote a German visitor. "The guts and other refuse are all thrown on the street and set up an unbearable stink." Waste disposal was simply a matter of tossing garbage and human filth out the window to rot; as a courtesy, the thrower cried "Heads up!" to alert pedestrians. To drown their sorrows, the poor drank cheap gin, a potent brew of 95 percent alcohol, a little water, and juniper berries "for taste." Gin shops advertised: "Drunk for a penny, dead drunk for tuppence." Each

William Hogarth's engraving Gin Lane, *depicting the ruinous effects of gin on London's poor. (1751)*

night, scores died of gin overdoses and in drunken brawls.[7]

The poor often rioted out of pure misery. Called the mobility by the rich—"mobs" for short—crowds rampaged everywhere. Astonished, Benjamin Franklin in 1769 described the mobility in action: "I have seen, within a year, riots in the country, about corn; riots about elections; riots about workhouses [in which poor people worked in exchange for bread]; riots [aboard] colliers [ships carrying coal]; riots of weavers; riots of coal-heavers; riots of sawyers; . . . riots of smugglers, in which custom house officers and excisemen have been murdered, the King's armed vessels and troops fired at."[8]

Since English cities did not have regular police forces but only part-time constables, panicky officials relied on the army to quell riots. A colonel, elegant in his tailored uniform, three-cornered hat, and shiny boots, would read the Riot Act, a law commanding the mob to disperse. Pocket watch in hand, he waited an hour, then ordered his soldiers (called redcoats because of their scarlet uniforms) to fire volley after volley into the mob. When the smoke cleared, he ordered a charge with fixed bayonets, the fourteen-inch blades at the end of the soldiers' muskets. Still, as Franklin noted, rioters might shoot back. In some riots, hundreds died and entire blocks of buildings went up in flames. However, since there were no fire departments, only volunteer groups, fires usually raged out of control until they ran out of fuel.

Paine lived near Covent Garden, a district of slums, gin taverns, and open-air markets. Each day, he passed hundreds of "ragged and hungry children, and persons

An eighteenth-century painting of redcoats attempting to quell a riot. (Date unknown)

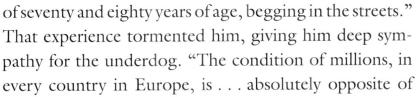

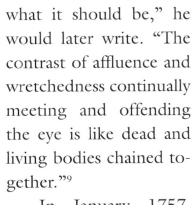

of seventy and eighty years of age, begging in the streets." That experience tormented him, giving him deep sympathy for the underdog. "The condition of millions, in every country in Europe, is . . . absolutely opposite of what it should be," he would later write. "The contrast of affluence and wretchedness continually meeting and offending the eye is like dead and living bodies chained together."[9]

In January 1757, the twenty-year-old suddenly quit his job and sailed aboard the privateer *King of Prussia* under Captain Edward Menzies. During the next eight months, the crew fought and captured seven French merchantmen. Paine never discussed his job on the ship or said whether he fought. We have no record of his ever having used violence toward another person. Anyhow, the voyage was a bonanza, his share of the

Astronomer James Ferguson, whose lectures Paine often attended at Covent Garden. (Date unknown)

spoils coming to £30. (£ is the symbol for pound sterling, a unit of English money.) That was more than his father earned in a year, worth about $25,000 in today's American money. Because he did not have to work for several months at least, he returned to London to further his education.

Paine rented a better room near Covent Garden. Each day, he spent hours seeing the sights and browsing the bookshops. Years later, he recalled that he especially liked to attend paid lectures by astronomer James Ferguson and mathematician Benjamin Martin. They inspired in him a lifelong interest in science. He became a human sponge, reading widely and absorbing facts easily. "I seldom passed five minutes in my life," he said, "in which I did not acquire some knowledge."[10]

Ferguson and Martin were Newtonians, followers of the chief founder of modern science. Sir Isaac Newton (1642–1727) was a genius who changed the way we think about the natural world. He did this by inventing a type of mathematics called calculus, discovering the secrets of light, and explaining gravity, the invisible force that binds the universe together. Universal gravitation, Newton's supreme law, holds that every bit of matter—from galaxies, stars, and planets to specks of dust—attracts every other body in exact mathematical proportions. In this way, the gravitational pull of the sun holds the planets in their orbits, just as Earth's gravity pulls an apple to the ground from a tree. Without gravity, the universe would, literally, fly apart.

Newton's findings suggested that things need not be as they were. Because his mathematical laws explained how the natural order worked, it followed that there must also be laws of social relations. Thus, human reason, the same God-given quality that solved the mysteries of nature, could also improve the human condition. Given enough knowledge, Newtonians believed, people could banish war, poverty, disease, and ignorance, in time creating a utopia, or perfect society. The Newtonian way of thinking strongly influenced young Paine. It gave him an enduring faith in the power of ideas. "An army of principles will penetrate where an army of soldiers cannot," he liked to say. "It will march on the horizon of the world, and it will conquer." That faith emboldened Paine to question all authority in his search for ways to create a better world.[11]

YEARS OF FAILURE

Meanwhile, Paine's life took a turn for the worse. As his prize money ran out, he set out on his own as a corset maker. Leaving London, he plied his trade in towns along England's east coast. In 1759, he met and married a lady's maid, Mary Lambert, a "pretty girl of modest behavior." Mary became pregnant, but she and her unborn child died the next year. We do not know how Paine took this double tragedy. We do know that afterward he sought a different line of work.[12]

Mary's father had been an exciseman, a low-level, low-paid civil servant. The exciseman's job was to collect the excise, a tax on imported goods, chiefly sugar, coffee, tea, tobacco, wine, and liquor. Shopkeepers were forced to add the excise to the prices they charged, harming sales and profits. To evade the tax, they bought from smugglers whenever possible. On moonless nights, ships landed cargoes, largely from Holland and France, on lonely east-coast beaches. From there, smugglers brought them by wagon to shops or sold them to consumers along the way. However, smuggling, like piracy, was a hanging offense. If they ran into excisemen, smugglers fought back with pistols and swords. Each year, around twenty excisemen died in the line of duty. Ignoring the danger, Paine applied for a job, passing the test in reading, writing, and arithmetic. In 1762, he took the oath of loyalty to His Majesty, By the Grace of God, King George III.

Things did not go well. In 1765, supervisors fired Paine for claiming to have inspected goods he never saw, a common offense among overworked excisemen. Returning to London, he scraped by on the small salary of a schoolteacher. Miserable, he wrote to beg the Excise Board's forgiveness, signing the letter "your honours' most dutiful humble servant THOMAS PAINE." The board forgave him and, after a long wait, in 1768 posted him to Lewes (pronounced "Lewis") in East Sussex, a county on the coast of the English Channel.[13]

Things improved. In March 1771, at age thirty-four, Paine married twenty-one-year-old Elizabeth Ollive, the daughter of a Lewes tobacco dealer. When his father-in-law died, he took over the shop, running it in his spare time.

Paine became a solid citizen (but not a voting one because he had no landed property), admired for his quick mind and writing ability. He wrote poems and articles for local newspapers—or at least historians *think* he wrote them, for authors often published under assumed names. As a member of the Headstrong Club, a group of civic-minded men who met in a local tavern, he debated the issues of the day. Club members thought him "a shrewd and sensible fellow," with an unusual "depth of political knowledge." One member celebrated his debating skills in a poem:

> *Immortal PAINE! while mighty reasoners jar,*
> *We crown thee General of the Headstrong War . . .*
> *Thy soul of fire must sure ascend the sky,*
> *Immortal PAINE, thy fame can never die.*[14]

Fellow excisemen respected Paine. Underpaid and risking their lives daily, they asked him to write something to convince Parliament to raise their salaries. The result was a pamphlet titled *The Case of the Officers of Excise*. In it, Paine argued that low wages led to corruption in the service because "Poverty . . . begets a degree of Meanness that will stoop to almost anything." Excisemen chipped in to have four thousand copies printed and to send the author to London. During the winter of 1772–1773, Paine gave copies to members of Parliament and others who might help the excisemen's cause. His mission accomplished nothing. Worse, his life began to fall apart.[15]

In April 1774, the Excise Board sacked Paine again, this time for leaving Lewes without permission. The tobacco shop failed, and he had to sell its contents and his household goods to settle his debts or else go to prison. His marriage collapsed for reasons he never explained. "It is nobody's business but my own," Paine growled when asked about the separation. "I had cause for it, but I will name it to no one." The couple never divorced; divorce was almost unheard of, requiring a private law passed by Parliament and bribes to legislators. Nor would the Paines ever meet again or remarry. Elizabeth moved in with her brother, scratching out a living as a dressmaker until her death in 1808. Occasionally, when he had a little extra money, Thomas sent her some, but without saying it came from him. We have no record of his having another romantic relationship after the breakup.[16]

Paine returned to London, not knowing what to do next. Luckily, a fellow exciseman knew Benjamin Franklin and introduced Paine to him. Now sixty-eight, Franklin was the most famous American of the day. A jack-of-all-trades, he had been a printer, a publisher, a postmaster, a scientist, and an inventor. He risked his life in an experiment to prove that lightning is electricity, and he invented the lightning rod to protect

Benjamin Franklin at his desk, surrounded by books and pamphlets, under the watchful gaze of a bust of Isaac Newton. (c. 1767)

buildings. In 1757, the Pennsylvania legislature sent him to London to look after the colony's interests. Franklin held the post during most of the next fifteen years, becoming the unofficial spokesperson for American concerns.

Paine told Franklin his tale of woe. He was desperate. He had no job, no property, no money, no prospects, and no hope. Franklin, a good judge of character, probably saw qualities in the former exciseman that others, perhaps even Paine himself, had missed. When Franklin suggested making a fresh start in America, Paine jumped at the offer.

To smooth the way, Franklin wrote a letter of introduction to his son-in-law Richard Bache (pronounced "Beech"), a wealthy Philadelphia merchant. "The bearer, Mr. Thomas Paine is . . . an ingenious worthy young man," Franklin noted. "If you can put him in a way of obtaining employment as a clerk, or assistant tutor in a school . . . you will do well, and much oblige your affectionate father."[17]

Franklin exaggerated. Life expectancy in eighteenth-century England was a little over thirty-six and a half years due in part to high infant mortality but also to poor hygiene and ignorance about the causes of disease. Thus, Paine, at thirty-seven, was hardly "young." No matter. The older man's personal recommendation told important people that he thought the newcomer deserving and that they should help him get settled.[18]

In October 1774, Paine sailed aboard the *London Packet*. He had no regrets about leaving the land of his birth, so bitter was he over the English social system and resentful of the high and mighty. As the ship headed west into the stormy Atlantic, the First Continental Congress was meeting in Philadelphia. Neither America nor Thomas Paine would ever be the same.

CHAPTER 2

The Great American Cause

*The great American cause owed as much to the
pen of Paine as to the sword of Washington.*

—Joel Barlow, American poet and diplomat, c. 1809

A WORLD OF TROUBLES

Crossing the Atlantic Ocean in a wooden sailing ship was not for the meek or
weak. The voyage was so dangerous that prudent travelers made their wills before setting out. Besides the menace of pirates and storms, ships swarmed with
vermin: rats, fleas, and lice. The worst threat was typhus, the dreaded "ship
fever," a highly contagious disease carried by human body lice. Once infected,
victims suffered splitting headaches, fierce skin rashes, high fevers, and often
death.

Typhus raced through the *London Packet,* killing five and sickening nearly
everyone else. Paine, burning with fever, was so weak he needed help to get

up to use the chamber pot. Fortunately, when the ship docked at Philadelphia on November 30, 1774, Dr. John Kearsley heard that a passenger with letters from Benjamin Franklin was aboard. The doctor had Paine hoisted ashore in a blanket and taken to his home, where he recovered over the next six weeks.

Next to London, Philadelphia was the largest and most prosperous city in the English-speaking world. Unlike London, the seaport of thirty thousand had hardly any poverty, thanks to its bustling overseas trade. Solidly built houses, thriving businesses, and busy craftsmen's shops lined the main streets. The city's wealthiest families dressed in finery imported from England and rode in luxurious carriages along unpaved streets that became seas of mud in heavy rainstorms.

The waterfront of Philadelphia in the eighteenth century. (c. 1770–1780)

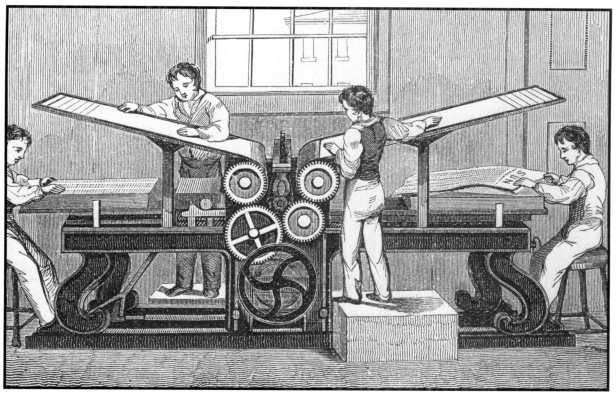

A woodcut of a man and his three apprentices setting type on a printing press much like the one Paine lived next to in Philadelphia. (Date unknown)

After recovering, Paine rented a room in a house at the corner of Market and Front streets, next to Robert Aitken's printing shop. Since most printing shops were also bookshops, Paine made himself at home. The owner, noticing a stranger browsing his shelves, struck up a conversation. One thing led to another, and Aitken offered Paine the job of editor of his latest venture, the *Pennsylvania Magazine.*

In the months that followed, Paine prepared other people's articles for publication and wrote pieces of his own. These ranged from scientific topics and the evils of dueling to "Reflections on Unhappy Marriages," a subject he knew only too well.

Paine also denounced slavery, which existed in all

thirteen colonies. Whenever he looked out the window of his room, he saw the Philadelphia slave market across the street. Every day except Sunday, the Lord's Day, dealers sold kidnapped African men, women and children to the highest bidder.

In an article titled "African Slavery in America," Paine attacked "the wickedness of the SLAVE-TRADE" and the hypocrisy of those who demand liberty for themselves while denying it to others. He wrote:

> *That some desperate wretches should be willing to steal and enslave men by violence and murder for gain is . . . contrary to the light of nature [and] to every principle of Justice and Humanity. . . .*
>
> *Too many nations enslaved prisoners they took in war. But to go to nations with whom there is no war, who have no way provoked . . . purely to catch inoffensive people, like beasts, for*

An ad announcing the sale of slaves—men, women, and children—in Charlestown (later known as Charleston), South Carolina. (July 24, 1769)

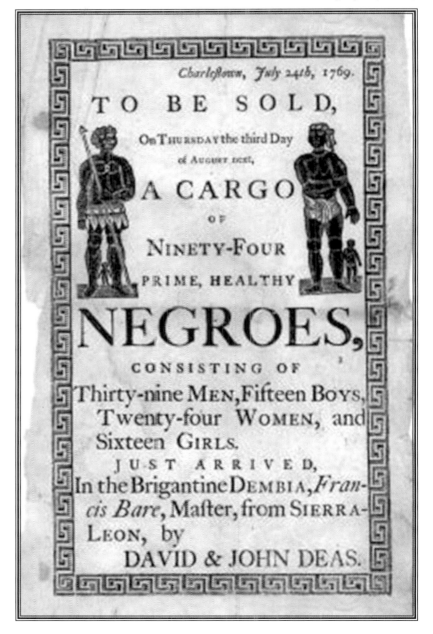

Charlestown, July 24th, 1769.

TO BE SOLD,

On THURSDAY the third Day of AUGUST next,

A CARGO OF NINETY-FOUR PRIME, HEALTHY NEGROES,

CONSISTING OF Thirty-nine MEN, Fifteen BOYS, Twenty-four WOMEN, and Sixteen GIRLS.

JUST ARRIVED,

In the Brigantine DEMBIA, *Francis Bare*, Master, from SIERRA-LEON, by

DAVID & JOHN DEAS.

slaves, is [the] height of outrage. . . . [So] many evils
[attend] the practice, as selling husbands away from
wives, children from parents, and from each other,
in violation of sacred and natural ties. . . .

If the slavery of the parents be unjust, much
more is their children's . . . [since] the children are
born free. . . . Certainly, one may, with as much
reason and decency, plead for murder, robbery,
lewdness and barbarity, as for this practice.[1]

When Benjamin Franklin, recently returned from England, founded America's first antislavery society, Paine eagerly joined.

The slavery issue soon faded for both men, as the quarrel between the colonies and England heated up. Having won the French and Indian War and seized Canada, England reacted with a combination of relief and arrogance. In the wake of victory, wrote Benjamin Franklin, "John Bull," the slang term for England, would likely "double his Fists and bid all the World to kiss his Arse." But victory had not come cheaply. In 1763, England's national debt stood at an all-time high of £140 million. Worse, now England would have to pay for the upkeep of troops needed to quell Indian uprisings on the frontier and prevent a French comeback.[2]

Where would the money come from? Surely not from the heavily taxed Englishmen. King George III's subjects complained about having to pay through the nose for nearly everything. Already they paid a tax on each windowpane, coach wheel, and candle they used. The salt that seasoned their food, and the powder they daubed on their wigs, was taxed. Tavern keepers had to fork over a few pence on every drink they served, whether imported or made locally, and barbers paid tax on every haircut and shave they gave. No wonder irate shopkeepers egged on mobs to riot against further taxes.

It seemed only fair that the king should ask Parliament to pass laws taxing the colonies for their own defense. However, colonists disagreed, saying they had already paid their fair share, in blood, to drive the French from Canada. Besides, they were taxed by their own elected assemblies, not a distant Parliament whose members they had never voted for and where they had no representatives.

In 1765, the year Paine lost his first job with the Excise Service, Parliament passed the Stamp Act. This was nothing new. For decades, the English had to buy special tax stamps for all legal documents, land deeds, mortgages, college diplomas, playing cards, calendars, newspapers, and pamphlets. Now Americans must pay, too.

They objected—vigorously. The cry "Taxation without representation is tyranny" echoed across the colonies. Local groups, calling themselves the Sons of Liberty, vowed not to buy English goods until Parliament came to its senses. More, they warned stamp-tax agents to quit their jobs. Those who refused found a straw man hanging outside their office or home with their name on it. As a result, Parliament backed down, repealing the Stamp Act within a year.

Tempers cooled, and in 1767 Parliament passed the Townshend Acts. Named for Treasury head Charles Townshend, these required colonists to pay a duty, or import tax, on various English goods: glass, lead, paint,

A depiction of colonists tarring and feathering a tax collector. (Date unknown)

paper, hats, and tea. The tea tax was especially irritating. Tea was a popular beverage, almost an addiction, in colonial America; people often drank as many as sixteen cups, heavily laced with sugar, at a sitting (think of what this must have done to bladders!). By taxing this "necessity," England reached into everyone's purse.

If Townshend thought colonists would meekly pay the duties, he was sadly mistaken. Again they boycotted English products. For good measure, the Sons of Liberty made it dangerous to be a tax collector. In public, they stripped tax collectors naked and covered them from head to foot with hot tar and feathers. Afterward, they paraded these bizarre "chickens" through the streets before jeering crowds.

Protests were especially violent in Boston. On March 5, 1770, redcoats fired into a howling, stone-throwing mob outside the Custom House, killing five, including a free black dockworker named Crispus Attucks. Patriots dubbed the killings the Boston Massacre and demanded an end to English "tyranny." This outraged people in England. Benjamin Franklin wrote,

The text underneath this illustration of the Boston Massacre reads: "Unhappy Boston! See thy Sons deplore, Thy hallowed Walks besmeared with guiltless Gore," and lists the names of those killed and injured. (c. 1770)

"Every man in England considers himself . . . a Sovereign over America . . . and talks about *our subjects in the Colonies.*" How dare "our subjects" protest! Nevertheless, Parliament gave in again, repealing all the Townshend duties but the one on tea, kept as a symbol of its right to tax the colonies in the future.[3]

The retention of the duty on tea only added fuel to the fire. If, colonists reasoned, Parliament could force taxation without representation down their throats, it might just as easily take away all their rights as Englishmen. In effect, they would become slaves, no different from the blacks sold at auction.

In December 1773, three tea ships arrived in Boston Harbor. When colonists tried to get them sent back to England, the governor of Massachusetts refused. So, during the evening of December 16, around a hundred Sons of Liberty, thinly disguised as Mohawk Indians, took matters into their own hands. Their song expressed their mood:

> *Rally, Mohawks! Bring out your axes,*
> *And tell King George we'll pay no taxes*
> *On his foreign tea.*[4]

Whooping and waving tomahawks, the "Mohawks" cracked open and dumped 342 tea chests overboard. In response to the "Boston Tea Party," Parliament passed several laws colonists called the Intolerable Acts because they were so severe. The acts, among other things, closed the port of Boston until the city paid for the tea and ordered more troops sent to keep order.

Colonists saw the Intolerable Acts as an intolerable

provocation. In September 1774, two months before Paine arrived, delegates from twelve of the colonies met in Philadelphia's Carpenters' Hall to discuss the crisis. During this First Continental Congress, they again voted to boycott English goods and halt the export of American goods to England. Before adjourning in late October, delegates decided to meet in a Second Continental Congress in May 1775, to evaluate the situation and discuss their next moves.

A month before the scheduled meeting, on April 19, 1775, fighting erupted when redcoats tried to seize weapons stored at Lexington and Concord, villages located about fifteen miles northwest of Boston. Worse followed as the Second Continental Congress assembled in Philadelphia. On June 17, the Sons of Liberty

An illustration of the Boston Tea Party, showing colonists dressed as Native Americans heaving tea into the harbor. (c. 1846)

and the redcoats fought a pitched battle at Breed's Hill, outside Boston. Mistakenly named the Battle of Bunker Hill, after an American position nearby, it was the bloodiest battle of the Revolutionary War, with more than a thousand redcoats and four hundred American patriots killed or wounded in a few hours. Congress responded by forming an army under a tall Virginian

Congress chose Virginian George Washington to lead the Americans in the Revolutionary War for his steadfast calm in the face of danger. (c. 1839)

named George Washington. Though he had never led an army in battle, the forty-three-year-old militia officer inspired confidence. He was, a delegate explained, "no harum scarum, ranting, swearing fellow, but sober, steady, and calm." America would need these qualities in the coming years.[5]

As fighting escalated, colonists asked serious questions. How far can we go? How far *dare* we go? There seemed only two choices. First: make a clean break; that is, turn the rebellion into a war for independence. Second: try to end the quarrel by persuading England to recognize their rights under the British constitution.

Those who urged a peaceful solution appeared to have the stronger case—or at least the *safer* case. Breaking away from the mother country, they warned, would be suicidal. Poorly armed, the colonists were no match for King George's army and navy. As if that were not bad enough, breaking away would cripple their foreign trade, impoverishing them while leaving them prey to France.

To urge independence also seemed shameful. Most colonists still saw themselves as English. They called England the homeland, in whose soil their family roots went back centuries. Colonists spoke English with English accents, thought in English, read English books and newspapers, and cooked English-style. Prominent leaders shuddered at the notion of separation. Thomas Jefferson wrote, "There is not in the British Empire a man who more cordially loves a union with Great Britain than I do." Despite the bloodshed, at dinners for his officers George Washington raised his wineglass and led the traditional Loyal Toast: "To the King!" When John Adams urged independence, delegates to the Second Continental Congress made him, he said, "an object of universal scorn."[6]

Thomas Paine thought the quarrel would end peacefully, until the fighting at Lexington and Concord changed his mind. "When the country, into which I had just put my foot, was set on fire about my ears, it was time to stir. It was time for every man to stir," he recalled later.[7]

One day, Paine struck up a conversation with Dr. Benjamin Rush in Aitken's bookshop. Going all out for independence now seemed the only sensible course, they agreed. Rush, age thirty, suggested that Paine write a pamphlet on the subject. Pamphlets were the fastest way to reach the widest audience. Because of the development of cheap, efficient printing in the late eighteenth century, mass propaganda became possible for the first time. Pamphlets—works of up to two hundred loosely sewn pages with paper covers—could be produced quickly and sold for a few pence each. Thus, the American

Dr. Benjamin Rush, who gave Paine the suggestion to write down his thoughts about American independence in a pamphlet. (c. 1802)

40

Revolution would become the first war waged both in print and on the battlefield. Rush would not write the pamphlet he suggested because he feared it might ruin his budding medical practice; Paine should write it instead, he said, for he was poor anyway and so had nothing to lose. Paine agreed. Though he wanted to title his work *Plain Truth*, Rush suggested *Common Sense*. So it was.

COMMON SENSE

The writing went slowly. Paine hunched over his papers, grasping his quill pen with ink-stained fingers, squeezing out each word. On January 9, 1776, Robert Bell, owner of a print shop on Third Street, pub-

COMMON SENSE;

ADDRESSED TO THE

INHABITANTS

OF

AMERICA,

On the following interesting

SUBJECTS.

I. Of the Origin and Design of Government in general, with concise Remarks on the English Constitution.

II. Of Monarchy and Hereditary Succession.

III. Thoughts on the present State of American Affairs.

IV. Of the present Ability of America, with some miscellaneous Reflections.

Man knows no Master save creating HEAVEN,
Or those whom choice and common good ordain.
THOMSON.

PHILADELPHIA;
Printed, and Sold, by R. BELL, in Third-Street.
MDCCLXXVI.

The title page of Common Sense. *(1776)*

lished the forty-six-page pamphlet at the price of eighteen pence. *Common Sense* appeared anonymously as "Written by an ENGLISHMAN." Little did the author think it would become an overnight sensation. America's first literary bombshell.

Paine set the tone in the opening sentence. In the spirit of the Enlightenment, he declared: "A long habit of not thinking a thing *wrong,* gives it a superficial appearance of being *right.*" In other words, age-old traditions are not proper guides to today's problems. Times change. Things change. What you always thought wrong might be right, and the other way around. So, dear reader, open your mind! Let me enlighten you with the facts! Then decide for yourself—and act![8]

Paine went on to list every argument against independence and stand it on its head. Monarchy, the former exciseman charged, was not sacred, as its defenders had taught for centuries. It came not from God, but was the "invention of the Devil." Of course, nobody could prove this. Yet, Paine realized, the colonists honored and respected England's kings. Only by shattering the image of monarchs as fathers of their people could he undermine loyalty to the present ruler, George III.[9]

Kings, Paine argued, originated as brutal thugs. If we traced kingship to its beginning in ancient times, "we would find the first of them nothing better than the principal ruffian of some restless gang, whose savage manners . . . obtained him the title of chief among plunderers." Together with their henchmen, absurdly called "nobles" and "aristocrats," these thugs seized territory. That done, they gave themselves grand titles like "Royal Majesty" and "Royal Highness" while oppressing the people they ruled.[10]

The author portrayed King George III as the latest in a long line of crowned bullies. He never even mentioned the royal name, as if writing it would soil his pages. Instead, he slammed "the Royal Brute of Britain" for having innocents murdered at Lexington and Concord. Afterward, the royal "wretch" calmly slept "with their blood upon his soul."[11]

But Paine exaggerated. George III was no brute, no wretch. Tall and blue-eyed, he loved his wife, Charlotte, who was said to have a face ugly enough to turn milk sour, and their fifteen children, whom he doted upon. Calling himself the Patriot King, he believed God had chosen him to rule with wisdom.

A portrait of King George III, who called himself "the Patriot King," while Paine dubbed him "the Royal Brute of England." (c. 1802)

Unfortunately, George III was not too wise. According to those who knew him well, His Majesty was "very obstinate," had an "inflexible temper," and lacked imagination. Once he got an idea, his mind locked onto it like a wolf trap. He said that wanting only the best for his people, he "must look on all who will not heartily assist me as bad men as well as ungrateful subjects." Having decided the colonies must pay for their defense, the king vowed to crush all resistance.[12]

Next Paine examined the economic case against independence. It made no sense. The British Empire, he declared, did not serve the colonists' interests. Being a part of it meant always getting dragged into European wars, sacrificing blood and treasure to others' whims, stupidity, and greed. America did not need the empire in order to prosper, because American products, Paine joked, "will always have a market while eating is the custom in Europe."[13]

As for challenging England's armed forces, Paine argued that America had vast untapped military resources: men to fight, timber for ships, and iron ore for making weapons. Besides, England was not the mother country, since mothers do not massacre their children. The facts—and simple common sense—pointed to one conclusion: "Everything that is right or natural pleads for separation. The blood of the slain, the weeping voice of nature cries, 'TIS TIME TO PART." The colonies should announce their departure with "a determined DECLARATION FOR INDEPENDENCE."[14]

Paine declared that instead of belonging to a foreign empire, independent America must be a democratic republic based on the people's choice of their government. That government must have a congress to make the laws and a president to enforce them. Their powers, in turn, must be clearly defined by a written constitution. The author called it the Continental Charter, or Charter of the United Colonies.

Finally, Paine raised the rebellion against royal power and taxes to a cause far greater than independence. He declared it a crusade for an idea. Appealing to his readers' idealism, he said they were fighting for unborn generations—for nothing less than the future of humanity. In words that fairly leaped off the printed page, he wrote:

> *The cause of America is in a great measure the*
> *cause of all mankind. . . . The sun never shined on a*
> *cause of greater worth. 'Tis not the affair of a city,*
> *a country, a province, or a kingdom. . . . 'Tis not the*
> *concern of a day, a year, or an age; posterity . . . will*
> *be more or less affected, even to the end of time, by*
> *the proceedings now. . . . O ye that love mankind! Ye*
> *that dare oppose not only the tyranny, but the tyrant,*
> *stand forth! Every spot of the old world is over-run*
> *with oppression. Freedom hath been hunted round*
> *the globe. Asia and Africa have long expelled her.*
> *Europe regards her like a stranger, and England*
> *hath given her warning to depart. O! receive*
> *the fugitive, and prepare in time an asylum for*
> *mankind. . . . We have it in our power to begin the*
> *world over again. The birth-day of a new world is*
> *at hand. . . .*[15]

The "power to begin the world over again"! Such words were not the concern of a day, a year, or an age. For in writing them, Paine became the champion of American exceptionalism, which is still a potent idea more than two centuries later. This holds that America is truly exceptional, different and special. Unlike other nations, it is supposed to be a model for the rest of humanity. As President Abraham Lincoln would tell Congress in December 1862, America is "the last best hope of earth." It has a sacred mission to advance liberty worldwide by its ideals and good example, thus abolishing the evils inherited from the past. The idea of American exceptionalism, however, has produced mixed results. It spurred the fight against slavery in the Civil War, and against tyranny in the two world wars of the twentieth century. But it also helped create disasters like the Vietnam War.

AMERICA SET ABLAZE

The appearance of *Common Sense* marked a turning point in two ways. Though he had not realized it when he began writing, the pamphlet ended Paine's voyage of self-discovery. For it gave him a mission he could never abandon. "I know but one kind of life I am fit for," he wrote, "and that is a thinking one, and, of course, a writing one." Paine became an author with a mission, an unswerving champion of liberty for all people. Above all, he got people to think. As he put it, "I am a Farmer of thoughts."[16]

Common Sense changed political writing, too. Until its appearance, authors aimed at influencing only the educated elite. Books had such titles as *The Rights of the English Colonies* and *The Genuine Principles of the English Constitution*. Authors argued calmly, politely, sprinkling their pages with Latin quotations from learned authorities. Paine did not wish to write in this way, nor could he. He wrote for the common people, those like him. To influence them, he had to grab their attention by appealing to their intelligence *and* to their emotions.

In his writings, a critic noted, Paine spoke "a language which the colonists had felt, but not thought of." He expressed their feelings in simple, vivid, anger-filled sentences. That anger, in turn, stemmed from his life experiences. The years of poverty, of seeing murderous laws carried out, of frustration with a society that allowed such inhumanity—all spilled onto the pages of *Common Sense*.[17]

The pamphlet spread like fire in dry grass. Within weeks of its publication, sales soared to over 150,000 copies; Paine gave his earnings to buy mittens for Washington's troops. Newspapers reprinted it free of charge. People read it in the privacy of their homes. Those unable to read had it read to them in taverns and workshops until the copies fell apart from wear. *Common Sense* also made its way across the Atlantic, translated into French, German, Danish, Spanish, and Polish. "Enlightened" Russians greeted it as "God's word." Empress Catherine the Great said it sent chills down her spine.[18]

Common Sense had a great effect on rebel leaders. George Washington admired its "sound doctrine and unanswerable reasoning," glowing praise from such a reserved man. Discontinuing the Loyal Toast, he ordered the pamphlet "read to all ranks." Thomas Jefferson called it "the simple voice of nature and reason." John Adams sent his wife, Abigail, a copy soon after it came off the press. "I could not have written any thing in so manly and striking a style," he admitted. Abigail declared herself "charmed" by the author's ideas. The future First Lady wondered how "an honest heart, one who wishes the welfare of his country and the happiness of posterity, can hesitate one moment at adopting them."[19]

The story of *Common Sense* illustrates the power of ideas to shape history. "Nothing but independence will

Abigail Adams, wife of John Adams, told her husband she was "charmed" by Common Sense. *(c. 1910–1920)*

go down," wrote Nicholas Cresswell, a Loyalist, or supporter of the king. "The devil is in the people." John Adams agreed. As he wrote Thomas Jefferson, "Every day rolls upon us independence like a torrent. . . . History is to ascribe the American Revolution to Thomas Paine."[20]

Congress appointed a five-man committee to draft a declaration of independence. Its members were Paine's friend Benjamin Franklin (Pennsylvania), John Adams (Massachusetts), Roger Sherman (Connecticut), Robert Livingston (New York), and Thomas Jefferson (Virginia). They chose Jefferson, at thirty-three the youngest member, to do the actual writing because he expressed himself so well.

Abigail Adams admired the tall, handsome redhead; she thought Jefferson looked "not unlike God." While Philadelphia sizzled in a summer heat wave, he set to work. Two weeks later, on July 2, 1776, he presented the final draft. After changing a word here and there, and cutting out a passage blaming George III for the slave trade, Congress issued the Declaration of Independence on July 4, which became the official birthday of the United States. The signers knew they were putting their lives on the line, for they had committed treason against England. "Well, gentlemen," Benjamin Franklin said half jokingly, "we must hang together or we shall most assuredly hang separately." Though the historic document reflected Paine's ideas, we have no evidence that he helped write it.[21]

The Declaration's most moving passage is the first sentence of the second paragraph: "We hold these

From left to right, Benjamin Franklin, John Adams, and Thomas Jefferson editing the Declaration of Independence. (c. 1921)

Truths to be self-evident, that all Men are created equal, that they are endowed by their Creator with certain unalienable Rights, that among these are Life, Liberty, and the Pursuit of Happiness." Unalienable rights are "natural rights," part of our humanity, because, like reason, they are God-given. The Declaration asserts that governments exist to secure these rights. Should

A painting by John Trumbull depicting the signing of the Declaration of Independence. (c. 1817–1819)

a government fail or, worse, oppress the people, the people may rightfully abolish it and create another. The rest of the document describes the colonies' grievances against George III, the personification of England.

The Declaration turned the Revolutionary War into the War for Independence. Wherever colonists gathered, it was read aloud. Abigail Adams wrote to her husband that when the people of Boston heard it, bells rang, cannons fired, and "every face appeared joyfull." On the North Carolina frontier, illiterate farmers chose a bright nine-year-old named Andrew Jackson as their "public reader." In his squeaky voice, the future seventh president read without "stopping to spell out the words." Elsewhere, people "killed" the king by de-

Colonists pulling down the statue of King George III in New York City. The statue was later melted and molded into musket balls for use in the war. (c. 1875)

stroying the symbols of royal authority. George III's coat of arms, on everything from churches to tavern signs, vanished overnight. In New York, a lead statue of the king on horseback stood on Bowling Green, near the southern tip of Manhattan Island. An eyewitness wrote that it "was taken down, broken into pieces, and its honor leveled with the dust." Patriots then molded the lead into forty-two thousand musket balls, intended "to assimilate with the brains of our infatuated [foolish] adversaries."[22]

*   *   *

WRITER AT WAR

While Paine was thrilled at the impact of *Common Sense*, he knew only hard fighting would make independence a reality. So he decided to help by joining the Pennsylvania Volunteers. Soldiers admired his gift for words; his army nickname was Common Sense. However, it soon became clear that their comrade was gun-shy. "Paine may be a good philosopher," one wrote, "but he is no soldier—he always keeps out of danger."[23]

General Nathanael Greene made him an aide, and they became friends. "Uncle Nat," as Washington called Greene, held Fort Lee, New Jersey, on the west bank of the Hudson River, opposite the northern tip of Manhattan Island. After forcing Washington's army out of New York, General Lord William Howe seized Fort Lee in a November 1776 surprise attack. The patriots' high spirits of July turned to despair with the onset of cold weather.

A portrait of General Nathanael Greene, or "Uncle Nat," as George Washington liked to call him. (c. 1785)

Washington led his defeated troops westward. It was awful. Driving rain turned roads into rivers of sticky, gooey mud. Everything was wet. Food ran

52

short. Hungry men shivered in threadbare uniforms; many walked barefoot, their shoes having worn out. Each day soldiers deserted, sometimes in whole companies, while terrified civilians pledged their loyalty to King George. At last, on December 13, Washington halted the retreat at the Delaware River, across from Trenton, New Jersey. Paine reached the camp a day or two later.

Washington admired the author of *Common Sense*. When they met, he told Paine he needed his pen more than his musket. Time was running out. The War for Independence was on its last legs. Unless Washington won a victory soon, resistance would collapse as patriots lost heart. He pinned his hopes on capturing Trenton from fierce German troops hired to fight alongside the redcoats. Germany in the 1700s was not a united country, but a crazy quilt of dozens of states, rich and poor, each with its own ruler, laws, government, and army. To raise cash, rulers of the poorer states rented soldiers to foreign countries for *Blutgeld* (blood money). Known as Hessians, because most came from the duchy of Hesse, some thirty thousand Germans fought for England.

To seize Trenton, Washington had to restore his army's confidence. Paine's job was to convince not only the troops but also all Americans that their cause was still worth fighting for. The author set to work immediately, writing by firelight on a drumhead in General Greene's tent. When nearly finished, he walked the thirty-five miles to Philadelphia, expecting a redcoat patrol to arrest him at any moment. By then, everyone knew he had written *Common Sense*. If captured, he could expect

The rearing pose of General Howe's horse in this portrait is intended to symbolize leading men into battle. (c. 1776–1790)

a court-martial followed by the gallows.

Paine reached Philadelphia eleven hours later. With General Howe's forces nearby, Congress had already fled, along with thousands of panicky residents. Paine stayed. He sat in his room, polishing *The American Crisis* and getting it ready for the printer. It was the first of thirteen pamphlets with the same title to appear during the war, each signed "COMMON SENSE." Published on December 19, 1776, copies reached Washington's camp four days later. They were just what the general needed.

The army waited in the moonlight; it dared not make fires, which would alert Hessian patrols across the river. As men huddled together, Washington had officers read *The American Crisis* to them. Its opening lines are the most powerful Paine ever wrote.

These are the times that try men's souls: The summer soldier and the sunshine patriot will, in this crisis, shrink from the service of his country; but he that stands it NOW, deserves the love and thanks of man and woman. Tyranny, like hell, is not easily conquered; yet we have this consolation with us, that the harder the conflict, the more glorious the triumph. What we obtain too cheap, we esteem too lightly: 'Tis dearness only that gives every thing its value. Heaven knows how to set a proper price upon its goods; and it would be strange indeed, if so celestial an article as FREEDOM should not be highly rated.[24]

If there was ever a time when the written word rallied spirits, it was in that dismal December of 1776. The impact of the first *Crisis* pamphlet outdid even that of *Common Sense*. Paine's words went to soldiers' hearts like fiery arrows. Ragged men, many with tears rolling down their cheeks, looked at one another in silent agreement. Their expressions said it all. Nobody could call *them* summer soldiers and sunshine patriots. Deep down they understood that they represented something new and wonderful: free people fighting for what they believed made life worth living.

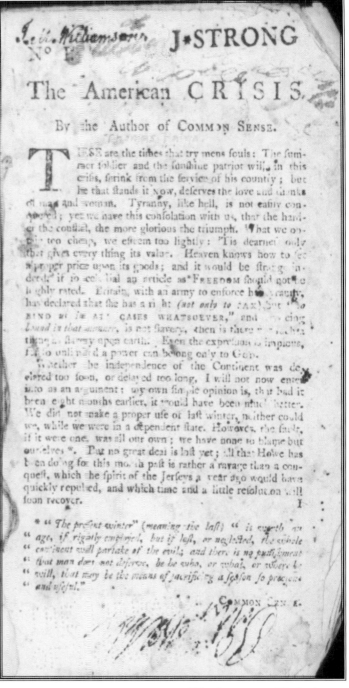

The first page of Paine's next pamphlet, The American Crisis. *(c. 1776)*

On the evening of Christmas Day, the army rowed across the Delaware and marched on Trenton. It was rough going. Now and then, the moonlight picked out red footprints in the white snow. The Hessians had enjoyed a riotous Christmas party, and most, including guards, were sleeping off the effects of too much *Schnaps*—strong liquor. At dawn the next day, December 26, they awoke to sounds of gunfire and shouts of "*These are the times that try men's souls!*" Caught by surprise, the Hessians surrendered. Washington had his victory. Afterward, recruits came to him by the hundreds. One said that "These are the times that try men's souls" was "in the mouths of everyone going to join the army."[25]

The capture of the Hessians at Trenton, New Jersey. (c. 1900–1912)

Paine issued the second *Crisis* pamphlet two weeks later, on January 13, 1777. In it, he told General Howe an unpleasant truth: Your royal master has set you an impossible task! America is so vast that it could swallow any invader. Paine's hero, George Washington, would make sure that "THE UNITED STATES OF AMERICA will sound as [proudly] in the world or in history as *The Kingdom of Great Britain*." Although the term United States of America was first used in the Declaration of Independence, Paine seems to have been the first to use it in a printed essay.[26]

Meanwhile, French leaders closely watched events in America. King Louis XVI and his ministers burned with shame over losing the French and Indian War. So, to get even, when the Revolutionary War began, they secretly sent Washington shiploads of military supplies. Yet, despite the Declaration of Independence, they refused to declare war, fearing the colonies might patch up their quarrel with the mother country. After Trenton, victories the next year at Princeton in New Jersey and Saratoga in New York erased their doubts. Certain that America was fighting "for keeps," France signed a formal treaty of alliance and declared war in May 1778. Benjamin Franklin led the three-member team that negotiated the treaty. Charmed by his wit and simple ways, crowds in Paris cheered the old man in the streets.

Meanwhile, Franklin's friend served the cause in various ways. Besides his writings, Paine became the secretary of Congress's Committee on Foreign Affairs and the clerk of the Pennsylvania General State Assembly. In February 1781, he joined Colonel John Laurens, a close friend of General Washington's, on a mission to seek more aid from France. Their ship, the *Alliance,* sailed into a swarm of drifting icebergs after leaving Boston. "The sea," Paine wrote, "in whatever direction it could be seen, appeared [an] assemblage of floating rolling rocks, which we could not avoid and against which there was no defense." Luckily, they made it through safely, arriving at the port of Lorient after a twenty-six-day voyage.[27]

Since Paine spoke no French, Elkanah Watson, an American traveler, became his interpreter. Watson immediately disliked Paine. Apparently, the success of *Common Sense* and the *Crisis* pamphlets had given the author a swollen head. "He was coarse and uncouth in his manners," Watson recalled, "and a disgusting egotist, rejoicing most in talking of himself"—an opinion shared by others over the years. Yet Watson was still grateful to him for influencing public opinion in favor of "the declaration of our Independence."[28]

After gaining a promise of more aid, Paine and Laurens sailed home aboard a French warship, reaching Boston on August 26, 1781. Final victory lay in sight. Five days earlier, Washington had begun his advance on the tiny port of Yorktown, Virginia. His goal: to win the war by trapping a large enemy force under the command of General Lord Charles Cornwallis. As American and French guns pounded Yorktown from the land, a French battle fleet prevented the garrison from escaping by sea. General Cornwallis surrendered on October 19, ending the fighting. As the redcoats left Yorktown, their bands played a catchy tune, "The World Turned Upside Down." So it had—for them.

Peace negotiations dragged on for nearly two years. Yet, Paine realized, America had won a stunning victory. He announced in the last *Crisis* pamphlet (April 19, 1783): "The times that tried men's souls are over— and the greatest and compleatest revolution the world ever knew is gloriously and happily accomplished." A peace treaty officially ended the war five months later.[29]

PAINE IN PEACETIME

Though victory delighted Paine, it depressed him, too. The war years had been the best of his life so far. He had served a cause he loved splendidly. His self-esteem had never been higher. But now he dreaded the future. He returned from France jobless and without any savings.

The surrender of the British forces led by General Cornwallis at Yorktown, Virginia, which ended the Revolutionary War. (c. 1870)

James Madison, friend to Thomas Paine, would go on to become the fourth president of the United States in 1809.

He had no family, no occupation other than political writing, and no head for business. "Trade I do not understand," he groaned. "Land I have none." Paine feared poverty, yes. More than anything, he feared becoming a nobody.[30]

Still, he had powerful friends, and none more so than George Washington. Paine had always come through for his adopted country, even giving it the profits from his writings, which would have made him rich. Washington wanted to reward his contribution. "Can nothing be done in our Assembly for poor Paine?" he wrote fellow Virginian James Madison. "Must the merits and services of *Common Sense* continue to glide down the stream of time, unrewarded by his country?" The Virginia General Assembly would not give a penny because the author had denounced its treatment of Native Americans and seizure of their lands.[31]

Washington refused to quit. He arranged to pay the author, out of secret funds used to pay spies, to write articles defending Congress's right to collect taxes in the states. Washington also persuaded the Pennsylvania legislature to award Paine £500. Next, at his urging, New York State gave a three-hundred-acre farm in New Rochelle, twenty miles north of New York City. Paine rented the land to a tenant farmer but kept the small cottage for himself. Finally, Washington convinced Congress to award him $3,000, a *very* generous sum back then. The money came just as Congress was discharging thousands of war veterans with IOUs, promises of back pay later, at a date not given.

Congress's gift, invested in U.S. government bonds, set Paine up for life. Expenses might be high at times, but he lived frugally, so he always had enough for basic needs. Freed of money worries, he could spend his time as he pleased.

Paine had always been interested in science. During the war, he worked unsuccessfully on a device for hurling firebombs across rivers. Now he turned to peaceful pursuits, inventing a "smokeless candle" and a motor powered by exploding gunpowder. Neither aroused any interest. Another invention, a bridge, was more practical. America's streams and rivers needed bridging. The only problem was that bridges had to rest on wooden piers, or supports, which were easily smashed during winter by blocks of ice carried downstream. To resist ice floes, Paine designed a single-span bridge made of separate cast-iron sections linked together. He called it "a child of Common Sense," a play on his nickname. It had thirteen sections, one for each state.[32]

Unfortunately, states rejected the project as too

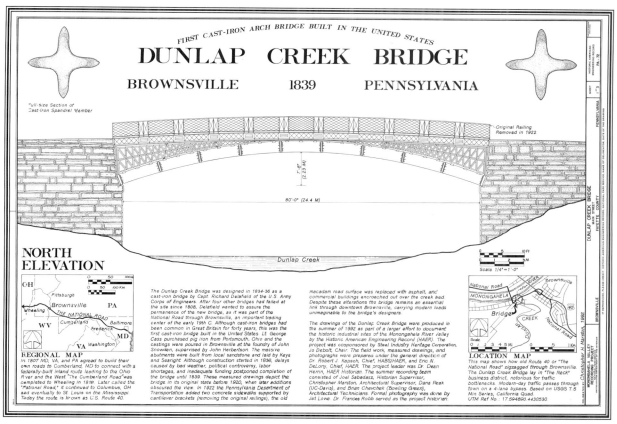

FIRST CAST-IRON ARCH BRIDGE BUILT IN THE UNITED STATES

DUNLAP CREEK BRIDGE

BROWNSVILLE   1839   PENNSYLVANIA

Full-size Section of Cast-Iron Spandrel Member

Original Railing Removed in 1922

7'-8" (2.23 M)

80'-0" (24.4 M)

NORTH ELEVATION

Dunlap Creek

Scale: 1/4" = 1'-0"

REGIONAL MAP
In 1807 MD, VA, and PA agreed to build their own roads to Cumberland, MD to connect with a federally-built inland route leading to the Ohio River and the West. "The Cumberland Road" was completed to Wheeling in 1818. Later called the "National Road," it continued to Columbus, OH and eventually to St. Louis on the Mississippi. Today the route is known as U.S. Route 40.

The Dunlap Creek Bridge was designed in 1834-36 as a cast-iron bridge by Capt. Richard Delafield of the U.S. Army Corps of Engineers. After four other bridges had failed at the site since 1808, Delafield wanted to assure the permanence of the new bridge, as it was part of the National Road through Brownsville, an important trading center of the early 19th C. Although cast-iron bridges had been common in Great Britain for forty years, this was the first cast-iron bridge built in the United States. Lt. George Cass purchased pig iron from Portsmouth, Ohio and the castings were poured in Brownsville at the foundry of John Snowden, supervised by John Herbertson. The massive abutments were built from local sandstone and laid by Keys and Searight. Although construction started in 1836, delays caused by bad weather, political controversy, labor shortages, and inadequate funding postponed completion of the bridge until 1839. These measured drawings depict the bridge in its original state before 1920, when later additions obscured the view. In 1922 the Pennsylvania Department of Transportation added two concrete sidewalks supported by cantilever brackets (removing the original railings), the old

macadam road surface was replaced with asphalt, and commercial buildings encroached out over the creek bed. Despite these alterations this bridge remains an essential link through downtown Brownsville, carrying modern loads unimaginable to the bridge's designers.

The drawings of the Dunlap Creek Bridge were produced in the summer of 1992 as part of a larger effort to document the historic industrial sites of the Monongahela River Valley by the Historic American Engineering Record (HAER). The project was cosponsored by Steel Industry Heritage Corporation, Jo Debolt, Chair. The field work, measured drawings, and photographs were prepared under the general direction of Dr. Robert J. Kapsch, Chief, HABS/HAER, and Eric N. DeLony, Chief, HAER. The project leader was Dr. Dean Herrin, HAER Historian. The summer recording team consisted of Joel Sabadasz, Historian Supervisor, Christopher Marston, Architectural Supervisor, Dana Peak (UC-Davis), and Brian Chevchek (Bowling Green), Architectural Technicians. Formal photography was done by Jet Lowe. Dr. Frances Robb served as the project historian.

LOCATION MAP
This map shows how old Route 40 or "The National Road" zigzagged through Brownsville. The Dunlap Creek Bridge lay in "The Neck" business district, notorious for traffic bottlenecks. Modern-day traffic passes through town on a 4-lane bypass. Based on USGS 7.5 Min Series, California Quad.
UTM Ref No.: 17.594890.4430530

Christopher H. Marston, 1992

The creators of this cast-iron arch bridge, still in service today, applied the building principles advocated by Paine in his design. (c. 1839)

expensive. Again Paine asked Benjamin Franklin for advice. Franklin's son, William, had been royal governor of New Jersey and had sided with England during the war. Devastated, his father never spoke to the "traitor" again. Instead, the old man saw Paine as a substitute, calling him his "adopted political son." Paine, in turn, regarded Franklin as his adopted father, discussing his writings and inventions with him.[33]

Franklin thought his "son" should try to sell his bridge in Europe. To help win support for the project, he gave Paine letters of introduction to the Royal Society in London, the world's foremost scientific organization. He also wrote Thomas Jefferson, now America's ambassador to France, asking him to introduce Paine to leaders of the Royal Academy of Sciences in Paris.

On April 26, 1787, fifty-year-old Thomas Paine sailed from New York. Though he planned to return by winter, it was not to be. Another revolution would keep him in Europe for fifteen years.

CHAPTER 3

The Peculiar Honor of France

It is to the peculiar honor of France that she now raises the standard of liberty for all nations, and in fighting her own battles, contends for the rights of all mankind.

—Thomas Paine, September 25, 1792

INTERESTING TIMES

"May you live in interesting times" is an ancient Chinese curse. Interesting times are abnormal times. They are troubled times of upheaval and danger, fear and woe. Yet the times did not seem very interesting when Thomas Paine arrived in France in the spring of 1787. The interesting part would come later, to his surprise, pleasure, and, finally, horror.

The author-inventor spent the next two years going back and forth between Paris and London. Despite Benjamin Franklin's letters and Thomas Jefferson's contacts, he found no backers for his bridge. He did however, learn that he had become a celebrity in England. His father had recently died, and his mother had mellowed over the years. Frances was so proud of her son that she fasted every July Fourth to honor his role in the "American war." Upon leaving Thetford, he arranged for her to receive a small allowance each year.[1]

Paine found that not all English politicians had supported the king's desire to crush colonial resistance. One, Irish-born Edmund Burke, became his friend, calling him "the great American," whose *Common Sense* "prepared the minds of the people for independence." Paine returned the compliment, praising Burke as "a friend of mankind." Pudgy and red-faced, Burke was a prominent orator, author, and reformer. A member of Parliament, he had for years denounced corruption and the bribery of lawmakers

Edmund Burke, member of Parliament, who called Paine "the great American." (c. June 1770)

with golden pills. When the colonies rebelled, Burke blamed the government for making them fight to defend their rights as Englishmen.[2]

While Paine made friends in England, France's interesting times began. Late-eighteenth-century France was not a happy place. Its society, like England's, resembled a pyramid, narrow at the top and broadening toward the base. Despite the similarity, however, there was a key difference between the two countries: privilege, the right to enjoy benefits and advantages legally denied to others. Unlike England, where the law applied to all, France held that certain Frenchmen were outside and above the law.

King Louis XVI stood at the top of the social pyramid. Described as a tenderhearted man, His Majesty was also dull and lazy, with little ability as a ruler; Thomas Jefferson labeled him a "fool." Louis XVI spent nearly all his waking hours tinkering with locks (his hobby) or hunting (his passion). Each year he shot thousands of birds and deer, just to beat the previous year's record. Nonetheless, he was "absolute." All power and all law came from the king. As he liked to say, "It is legal because it is my will." His Majesty made the law, though he was not accountable to it.[3]

Since France had nothing like habeas corpus, Louis XVI could jail anyone without pressing charges in a court. All he had to do was write the person's name on a *lettre de cachet*—arrest order—and officers took that person to a royal prison. There the man or woman remained "at the King's pleasure," even for life. France's most famous, and most dreaded, prison was the Bastille, a walled fortress looming over the center of Paris.

Beside the king stood Queen Marie Antoinette, an Austrian princess married at the age of fifteen. Badly educated, Her Majesty could scarcely write her own name. A vain person, she spent fortunes on jewels and clothes, buying three or four expensive dresses every week, and she gambled recklessly. Easily bored, she and her favorite court ladies whiled away their days playing dairymaid and shepherd in a miniature farm village she had built on the grounds of one of the royal palaces. Her brother, Austrian emperor Joseph II, had a low opinion of his sister and brother-in-law. "Together," he growled, "they are a couple of awkward nincompoops." Even so, the queen would later face the terrors of the French Revolution with dignity and courage.[4]

Below the royal family were the Estates, the three classes to which France's twenty-six million people belonged. The five-hundred-thousand-odd members of

Marie Antoinette with her husband, King Louis XVI of France (right), and her brother Archduke Maximilian Franz of Austria (left). (c. 1775–1777)

67

the combined First and Second Estates included the clergy of the Roman Catholic Church, the official state church, and the aristocracy. Members of these Estates had the privilege of paying no taxes. Clergymen did, however, assemble every five years to vote "free gifts" to the king. Only Catholic religious ceremonies could be conducted in public; Protestants and Jews had to conduct theirs in private. The Catholic clergy also controlled education and banned any books they judged unchristian, or "dangerous to morals." Favored nobles, as members of the Second Estate, lived like royalty, in rambling country houses called châteaus staffed by hundreds of servants.

All other Frenchmen, around 95 percent of the population, belonged to the Third Estate. This included people as varied as peasants and townspeople: merchants, manufacturers, shopkeepers, doctors, lawyers, artisans, laborers, the unemployed, and the poor. Being of "low birth," they had no privileges at all. Taxes were collected, wars declared, and laws made without their consent.

During the 1780s, a mood of defiance took hold in France. Nothing reflected this mood better than *The Marriage of Figaro,* a comedy by Pierre-Augustin Caron de Beaumarchais, first acted in Paris in 1784. In this daring attack on the privileges of the nobility, Figaro, the hero, a barber, dresses down an insolent count. "No, My Lord Count," says he. "Because you are a great nobleman you think you are a great genius. . . . Nobility, fortune, rank, position! How proud they make a man feel! What have *you* done to deserve such advantages? Put yourself to the trouble of being born—nothing more! For the rest—a very ordinary man!" Though the play scandalized the nobility, it became a hit, earning more than any other French play of the time. Before long, an anonymous cartoon also began to make the rounds. It showed a priest and a nobleman riding on the back of a ragged commoner. The caption read: "THE GAME MUST END SOON."[5]

So it did. Resentful of privilege and made desperate by high taxes, mass unemployment, crop failures, and soaring bread prices, the common people grew ever more restless. In 1789, their anger erupted like a volcano.

A 1789 French cartoon, titled "The Game Must End Soon," depicting a clergyman and a nobleman riding on the back of a peasant.

Trouble began on July 14, ten weeks after George Washington took the oath of office as our first president. That afternoon, a mob stormed the Bastille, freeing the few prisoners it held, killing its commanders. and carrying their severed heads around Paris on long spears called pikes. Louis XVI was clueless. Awakened at two

BASTILE

A correct View of the Bastile, with its Ground Plan.

An illustration of the Bastille (with its floor plan) being besieged by revolutionaries on July 14, 1789. Bastille Day is still celebrated on July 14. (Date unknown)

o'clock the next morning, he muttered to an aide, "Is it a revolt?" The aide replied, "No, Sire, it is a revolution!"[6]

The French Revolution, once it began, steadily grew in violence. In the weeks after July 14, peasants went on a rampage, burning nobles' châteaus, while the urban poor looted food shops. "Death to the rich!" they chanted. "Death to the aristocrats!" Anyone they disliked, or who happened to be at the wrong place at the wrong time, met a ghastly end. Mobs howling *À la lanterne!*" (To the lamppost!) hanged victims from the tall lampposts that stood at the corners of Paris's main streets.[7]

Meanwhile, representatives of the Third Estate, who were chiefly lawyers by profession, formed the National Assembly. On August 26, it issued the Declaration of the Rights of Man and the Citizen. Modeled on the Declaration of Independence, it announced, "Men are born and remain free and equal in their rights." Government exists to protect the "natural rights" of man. "These rights are liberty, property, security, and resistance to oppression." A few days later, the assembly abolished all privileges in France.[8]

The news from Paris rocketed across Europe. Millions greeted "the dawn of universal liberty" with cheers and fireworks. Oh, the joy! Oh, the thrill! Oh, to be young in 1789! English poet William Wordsworth could hardly contain his emotions:

> Bliss was it that dawn to be alive,
> But to be young was very heaven! . . .
> When Reason seem'd the most to assert her rights,
> . . . to assist the work,
> Which then was going forward in her name.
> Not favor'd spots alone, but the whole earth . . .

Not to be outdone, German university students hailed the Declaration with raised beer glasses and cries of *"Freiheit!"* (Freedom!). In Holland, people marched through the streets shouting France's revolutionary motto, *"Liberté, Égalité, Fraternité"* (Liberty, Equality, Fraternity [Brotherhood]).[9]

For Thomas Paine, the French Revolution was a personal triumph, a logical result of his writings and the War for Independence. When the Marquis de Lafayette, a former aide to George Washington, asked Paine to send the president the key to the Bastille as a memento, his heart "leaped with joy." The key is still on display at Washington's home, Mount Vernon, in Virginia.[10]

Yet Paine's English friend Edmund Burke was deeply troubled. At first, Burke called the fall of the Bastille a

The Great MONSTER, REPUBLICAN, having traversed great part of EUROPE and "shed his blessings all around," animated by a desire to Enlighten all mankind, degins even to grant those Blessings to a Nation of Pirates. — But see BRITANIA has roused her LION to give this Monster, a PROPER RECEPTION.

A political cartoon showing France as a monster, with one foot on Switzerland, facing Great Britain, saying, "All de Nations in Europe has accepted de Liberty, la François. . . . Me will come and plant de Tree of Liberty in your Hearts & make your Nation free."
(April 9, 1798)

"wonderful spectacle." What next? Paine thought he knew. The French Revolution, he wrote from Paris, "is surely the forerunner of other revolutions in Europe." How wonderful! In copying America's example, France had ignited a movement Paine hoped would sweep away all monarchies in favor of democratic republics. In this, however, he was naïve, with too simple a view of events. His mistake was to think that France was repeating the American experience. But it was not. This is because the experiences of one country, with all its history and traditions, can never be transferred to a different one.[11]

Paine's optimistic attitude shocked Burke. Like

most Englishmen, he had no love for France, an enemy since the Middle Ages. Since the mid-1300s, the two countries had fought many wars, including the agonizingly long Hundred Years' War and, most recently, the struggles over American independence. However, the French Revolution was no ordinary conflict over territory, wealth, or national honor. As it unfolded, Burke sensed something had gone horribly wrong. He felt things would spin out of control, leading to the breakdown of order in France and a savage war across all Europe. Time would prove him a prophet.

Like Thomas Paine, many people compared the French Revolution to the American Revolution; many still do. After all, both were products of Enlightenment ideals of natural rights. Beyond that, however, they had little in common.

The main goal of America's revolutionaries was to break away from a foreign empire. They did not wish to export their revolution abroad, and surely not by military force. Nor did they hope to create a "perfect" society by destroying the prewar social order. In the young republic, the well-to-do, the well-connected, and the well-educated controlled the state governments, as they had the colonial legislatures. The Founders' main challenge was bringing thirteen quarreling states, peacefully, into a united nation under a constitution. Though there were ferocious political battles, American politics was not a game of winners take all and losers die. With one exception, the Founders died in bed, of natural causes. Only the brilliant Alexander Hamilton, George Washington's military secretary and later first secretary of the

Treasury, met a violent end. Vice President Aaron Burr killed him in a pistol duel over a private matter.

The French Revolution took another course, as we will soon see in detail. It was more radical because its leaders were impatient, driven by their wish to turn Enlightenment ideals into reality. Extremists, they aimed at the immediate and total transformation of society—at all costs. They expected success would lead to paradise on earth. To reach this marvelous end, they felt they must make a clean break with the past. This was possible only by overthrowing the old system of government, the nobility, and the Catholic Church. Naturally, such radical ideas provoked opposition. Opposition led to civil war and state terror against any who thwarted, or might thwart, the revolution leaders' program. Even opposition in thought and feeling became a capital crime. Nevertheless, extremists echoed philosopher Jean-Jacques Rousseau in their belief that the French people must be "forced to be free."[12]

BATTLE OF THE BOOKS

To alert England to the dangers he saw looming ahead, Burke wrote *Reflections on the Revolution in France*. Like Paine's *Common Sense*, it ranks high among the classics of political writing. Published in November 1790, it has enjoyed a long life. During the twentieth century, it did much to inspire the conservative movement in America. Still in print, it is read in college history and political science courses. The University of Chicago and several other major universities have Edmund Burke Societies, which discuss and debate his political ideas and their ongoing significance.

Burke thought the American and French revolutions had nothing in common. As a member of Parliament, we recall, he had supported the rebellious colonists. In two famous speeches, "On American Taxation" (1774) and "On Conciliation with America" (1775), he roundly condemned the abuses of King George III's government. Americans, he insisted, were not wild-eyed fanatics, but sensible people deeply wronged. They did not seek to remake the world, except by encouraging others with their good example. They only wanted to enjoy what had always been theirs under English law.

Burke disagreed with the Declaration of Independence in one respect. For some reason, however, he had not raised the matter during the American Revolution. Now, in *Reflections on the Revolution in France,* he rejected the idea of natural rights granted by God. These rights, he declared, did not exist. They were fantasies, creations of

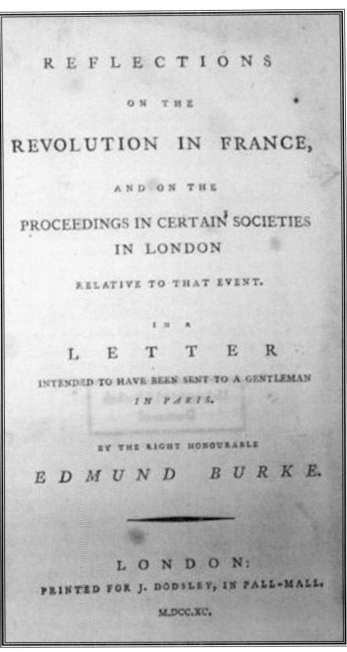

REFLECTIONS

ON THE

REVOLUTION IN FRANCE,

AND ON THE

PROCEEDINGS IN CERTAIN SOCIETIES
IN LONDON

RELATIVE TO THAT EVENT.

IN A

L E T T E R

INTENDED TO HAVE BEEN SENT TO A GENTLEMAN
IN PARIS.

BY THE RIGHT HONOURABLE

E D M U N D   B U R K E.

LONDON:
PRINTED FOR J. DODSLEY, IN PALL-MALL.
M.DCC.XC.

Though a fan of Common Sense, *Edmund Burke wrote* Reflections on the Revolution in France *to highlight the danger of attempting to follow in America's footsteps.* (c. November 1790)

"men of theory" and "desperate adventurers in philosophy," ignorant of the real world. According to Burke, rights come from society and nowhere else. His study of history showed that every society devises ideas, laws, and ways to meet its particular needs. Of course, these differ from place to place. That any society still exists after many centuries proves its "ancient opinions and rules of life" right *for it*. History, in effect, had blessed them, so we the living must cherish them. If not, we risk chaos.[13]

Of course, Burke realized that all societies must change to meet fresh challenges. Yet, he thought, their members should move ahead with care, changing only what they absolutely must, and that very gently. They must "approach the faults of the state as to the wounds of a father, with pious awe and trembling solicitude." More, they should "look with horror on those children of their country, who are prompt rashly to hack that aged parent to pieces . . . in hopes they may renovate their father's life." In short, when making changes, take it easy and go slowly and not too far, or you will wreck the society.[14]

Society, Burke continued, is more than a matter of profit and loss in business, "or some such low concern." It is "a partnership not only between those who are living, but between those who are dead, and those who are to be born." It followed that drastic changes of the sort Paine and the French revolutionaries wanted would open the floodgates, causing worse abuses than they aimed to correct.[15]

Burke distrusted human nature, believing we are

creatures of emotion no less than reason. Emotion is a powerful, but dangerous, quality. While it may energize us to resist evil, it can easily overcome reason. Mobs are naturally prone to emotion; that is why he called the uneducated the "swinish multitude." When emotion takes hold of a mob, its members literally act like selfish pigs. By challenging the existing social order, Burke said, the French Revolution had unleashed the demons of unreason: fear and panic, rage and hatred. As a result, "there must be blood."[16]

The shedding of blood inevitably leads to chaos, and chaos to military dictatorship. Burke thought of armies as tigers in a circus, beasts obedient only to strong masters. He predicted that in the chaos of revolution, a popular general "who possesses the true spirit of command, shall draw the eyes of all men upon himself. Armies will obey him on his personal account. . . . But the moment in which that event shall happen, the person who commands the army is your master." Burke's prediction came true with Napoleon Bonaparte, a military genius and the first modern dictator.[17]

Publication of *Reflections on the Revolution in*

Less than fifteen years after Burke's warning of a military dictatorship, Napoleon Bonaparte crowned himself the emperor of France. (Date unknown)

France triggered a war of words in England. No fewer than 250 books and pamphlets appeared to support or challenge its ideas. The most effective challenge came from another Thomas Paine masterpiece. Dedicated to George Washington and titled *Rights of Man,* it was published, in two parts, in February 1791 and February 1792. In it, the author took pride in being a free man, a lover of truth and humanity. "Independence is my happiness, and I view things as they are. My country is the world, and my religion is to do good."[18]

Calling Burke's work an "outrage" filled with "ignorance" and "horrid principles," Paine defended the French Revolution as just and necessary. He began by explaining away its early violence. That arose, he claimed, not from the madness of mobs but from the bad example set during centuries of royal absolutism. Anyhow, nothing could change the fact that the Revolution was "the tremendous breaking forth of a whole people" freeing themselves from tyranny. Now things would surely calm down, the author predicted. Again he was wrong, as time would tell.[19]

Paine argued that natural rights are real, because they, along with reason, are the God-given basis of our humanity. More, he urged readers to ignore outmoded traditions such as the British constitution. The dead are dead, so let them rest in peace. Whatever may have worked for them cannot bind the living forever.

> *Every age and generation must be free to act for itself,* in all cases. . . . *Man has no property in man; neither has any generation a property in the generations, which are to follow. . . . Every*

generation is, and must be, competent to all the
purposes which its occasions require. It is the living,
and not the dead, that are to be accommodated. . . .
I am contending for the rights of the living *. . . and*
Mr. Burke is contending for the authority of the
dead over the rights and freedom of the living.[20]

As Paine warmed to his subject, he repeated arguments from *Common Sense* almost word for word. Monarchy "is in its nature tyranny," the source of all human

This English cartoon critical of Thomas Paine shows him holding Rights of Man, *surrounded by injustices and standing on labels (representing morals), defending the extreme measures taken in revolutionary France and appealing to the English to overthrow their monarchy.* (December 26, 1792)

misery, and aristocracy a "monster." The idea of hereditary rulers leaving their offices to their heirs was "as absurd as an hereditary mathematician, or an hereditary wise man." Rational people judge others by their character, intellect, and achievements, not by their fathers' titles. Nevertheless, overthrowing privilege could not, by itself, create the good society.[21]

Paine broke new ground by arguing that true liberty requires freedom from want. Hungry people cannot be free people because they are slaves to their stomachs. Hunger forces them to obey those who offer a morsel of food, however evil they may be. Thus, to promote freedom, Paine outlined a program to correct the abuses he had seen in England. His program called for abolishing "irrational and tyrannical laws" that had children hanged for petty offenses. It also looked forward to what we today call the welfare state: free education, unemployment benefits, old-age pensions, and public housing. The money to pay for these programs, Paine noted, could easily come from a progressive tax; that is, those who earned more, paid more taxes. In 1797, Paine wrote *Agrarian Justice,* a more detailed plan for social reform.[22]

For Paine, another European age began with the fall of the Bastille. "It is an age of Revolutions, in which every thing may be looked for." An optimist, he expected revolutions to spread from France across the Continent, then worldwide, bringing eternal peace under a world republic ruled by a world government. Humanity would then live in an earthly paradise, happily ever after, he thought. However, he did not reckon with the tenacity of those whose way of life depended on the old order. As we will see, they would fight tooth and nail to keep "the French disease" from spreading.[23]

CRACKDOWN

There had never been anything like *Rights of Man*. Within a decade, it sold over a million and a half copies, more than any book in history except the Bible. This was no accident. Like *Common Sense*, it expressed feelings that most people who read it, or heard it read aloud, could not articulate in their own words. For radicals, those favoring drastic changes, it was a call to action. An anonymous poet caught their spirit:

> *Prepare, prepare . . .*
> *Freedom cheers the brow of care;*
> *The joyful tidings spread around.*
> *Monarchs tremble at the sound!*
> *Freedom, freedom, freedom, freedom—*
> *The Rights of Man, and Paine resound!*[24]

In England, radicals seized on *Rights of Man* as if it were written by the hand of God. Corresponding societies sprang up to share information, as they had in America before the Revolution. In towns and cities, radicals demanded a written constitution and votes for all men (but not women). More alarming to the aristocracy, people openly disrespected their social superiors, including George III. Once, a crowd shouting "No king!" greeted His Majesty as his gilded coach rolled through London.[25]

Paine's book seemed the devil's work to England's

A cartoon showing the London Corresponding Society, "alarm'd," sitting beneath a portrait of "Tom Payne." (c. 1798)

upper classes. Even critics of the king saw *Rights of Man* as unleashing a monster. "If," said one, "Mr. Paine should be able to rouse up the lower classes, [there] will probably be . . . wild work, and all we now possess, whether in private property or public liberty, will be at the mercy of a lawless and furious rabble." Faced with that menace, Prime Minister William Pitt cast aside ancient liberties to prevent what he called "the total subversion of the established form of government."[26]

The prime minister cracked down with all the brutality born of fear. Government spies joined radical societies like the Robin Hood Club, reporting members' names to the authorities. Government agents, the infamous "book police," raided bookshops, seized Paine's writings, and burned them in town squares. People who printed or sold Paine's books got fined for the first offense, had their shops closed for the second, and went to jail for the third. Soldiers dragged especially annoying speakers, printers, and booksellers aboard ships bound for Australia, a penal colony on the other side of the globe. Paine protested the crackdown in a public letter, saying it was "dangerous [for] any government to say to a nation, *'thou shalt not read.'*"[27]

An English cartoon showing "Tommy Paine," the "little American Taylor," measuring the Crown for "a new Pair of Revolution Breeches." (May 23, 1791)

The crackdown intensified. Attacks on Paine grew nastier. Pitt's agents hired hack writers to dig up dirt on Paine; when they found none, they used their imaginations. Hacks accused "Mad Tom" of being a thief and an unfaithful husband. Bad poets wrote bad poems. One went:

> Old Satan had a darling boy
> Full equal he to Cain
> Born peace and order to destroy
> His name was—Thomas Paine.

Wearing boots with hobnails engraved T.P. became the fashion among the wealthy, so they could trample on the man and his ideas with their every step.[28]

Before long, attacks with words turned into attacks with clubs. Government-paid "Church and King" mobs beat up radicals and trashed their homes. Riots against *Rights of Man* erupted in some three hundred towns across England. Mobs hanged the author in effigy, making him fear for his life whenever he ventured onto a London street. One day, a friend, poet William Blake, warned, "You must not go home, or you are a dead man." Somehow, Blake had learned that paid assassins were out to get Paine.[29]

Rather than stop a bullet, Paine fled. On September 14, 1792, he sailed from Dover, bound for the French port of Calais. He nearly didn't make it. Only by showing a personal letter from George Washington did he persuade suspicious English customs officials to let him board the ship. Meanwhile, a crowd had gathered at dockside. As the ship raised anchor, people hurled curses and stones at its famous passenger. Twenty minutes later, a messenger rode into Dover with a warrant for Paine's arrest.[30]

France gave him a hero's welcome, with cries of

"*Vive Thomas Paine!*" (Long live Thomas Paine!), cheers, and, according to custom, kisses—lots of kisses from both men and women. While Paine never learned to speak French, *Rights of Man* spoke for his goodwill. In August, a month before Paine fled from England, he had been made an honorary French citizen by the National Convention, the body charged with drawing up a constitution.

When he arrived, voters elected *Citoyen Paine* (Citizen Paine) to the National Convention. It was a good thing, too. For, in his absence, a London jury found him guilty of sedition—speaking or acting to incite rebellion against the government. Paine replied by damning England's government as a "great, if not the greatest, perfection of fraud and corruption that ever took place since governments began."[31]

Paine vowed to overthrow that hateful crew. In years to come, he urged French leaders to make a "descent on England," to invade the land of his birth. Based on his experience in the Excise Service, he recommended landing sites along the coast for French troops and artillery. "The intention of the expedition was to give the people of England an opportunity of forming a government for themselves," he explained. However, Paine did not say what would happen if they rejected the "opportunity" offered by foreign invaders.[32]

THE REIGN OF TERROR

Paine soon realized that he'd leaped from the English frying pan into the French fire. For he arrived just as the

Another English cartoon showing Britannia (Great Britain) clasping the trunk of a large oak while Thomas Paine tugs with both hands at her corset, trying to crudely reshape her according to his wishes. (c. 1793)

Revolution entered its most violent phase, demonstrating brutality he had not imagined possible. In America, Paine had known about violence between Patriots and Loyalists. It was especially vicious in the South, where Loyalists joined redcoats in shooting enemies after they surrendered, and while they begged for mercy. However, even in the South, there were no mass executions staged to entertain jeering spectators.

Although Europe had seen other revolutions before, these never spread beyond a single country, nor had their leaders meant for them to. The French Revolution was different. Like Paine, its supporters hoped to sweep away the old order in a glorious crusade for *"Liberté, Égalité, Fraternité."* Hardly a day passed in the National Convention without cries of *"Mort aux tyrans"* (Death to the tyrants). Said Jacques-Pierre Brissot, a leading member, "We cannot be calm until all Europe is in flames."[33]

Europe's rulers felt they had no choice. Either they went under or they waged their own crusade against the Revolution's "poisonous doctrines." Their war preparations, in turn, further provoked the revolutionaries. Finally, in April 1792, the National Convention declared a "war of peoples against kings" by attacking Austrian-controlled Belgium. Austria found allies in England, Holland, Spain, and Prussia, which was the most powerful of the independent states that made up Germany at the time.

The foreign forces, better armed and led, easily won the opening battles, invading France itself. The invasion had the effect of throwing a torch into a barrel of gunpowder. Its explosion ignited a panic in Paris, as roving bands of sansculottes began seizing nobles, priests, and others suspected of favoring the enemy. So called because the men wore trousers instead of the knee breeches (*culottes*) and silk stockings favored by the wealthy, the sansculottes were militant workers, shopkeepers, and the poor. As the enemy advanced, frenzied mobs filled the air with "Ça ira!" ("It'll Be Fine!"), a terrifying song set to a popular dance tune:

A typical *sansculotte. His clogs and pants (as opposed to knee breeches, or* culottes*) indicate that he is not a nobleman, but a commoner. (Date unknown)*

Ah! It'll be fine, it'll be fine, it'll be fine
The aristocrats to the lamppost
. . . we'll hang them!
If we don't hang them
We'll break them
If we don't break them
We'll burn them. . . .
Ah! It'll be fine, it'll be fine, it'll be fine
Equality will reign everywhere. . . .

The aristocrats, we'll hang them!
And when we have hung them all
We'll stick a shovel up their arse.[34]

During the September Massacres (September 2 to 7, 1792), sansculottes stormed five Paris prisons and murdered thirteen hundred inmates, including 225 Catholic priests, with clubs, knives, and meat cleavers. The blood had scarcely dried in the streets when Paine reached the capital a week later. On September 20, French forces narrowly defeated the invaders, saving Paris and restoring a measure of calm.

The big question when Paine arrived was what to do about the king. Louis XVI had pretended to accept the Revolution while plotting against it. As the war began, he secretly wrote the Austrians, pressing them to invade his country and crush the Revolution. When a locksmith reported that His Majesty had a hidden safe, guards broke it open and found copies of his letters. The National Convention immediately abolished the

A sansculotte killing a nobleman during the September Massacres. (c. 1792)

monarchy, declared France a republic, and charged the former king with treason.

During the trial, Paine, the hater of monarchy, urged mercy. Speaking slowly to allow the translator to keep up, he voted Louis guilty of treason. Yet he continued, "As France has been the first of European nations to abolish royalty, let her also be the first to abolish the punishment of death." Let France jail the disgraced king until the war ended, then send the royal family into exile in the United States. Executing Louis would just make the enemy fight harder, while angering the Americans, who were still grateful for his help in winning their independence.[35]

The National Convention approved the death penalty by a single vote. Like so much else in France, the method of execution had, until then, depended on the victim's social class. Traditionally, nobles found guilty of a capital crime died "honorably," beheaded swiftly with a sword or ax. Commoners died "dishonorably" by hanging, often slowly and painfully as the noose choked them. On January 21, 1793, the disgraced king died "democratically" by a novel method.

Named for its inventor, Dr. Joseph Guillotin, the guillotine was a beheading machine designed to execute people of all classes the same way. The device had two fourteen-foot posts and an eighty-eight-pound blade, razor sharp, set in grooves between them and raised by a pulley. The masked executioner tied the condemned to a board, secured the person's neck in a wooden collar, and released the pulley. Down came the blade with a force of 888 pounds per square inch. "The head flies

HELL BROKE LOOSE, OR, THE MURDER OF LOUIS.

The "democratic" execution of Louis XVI, surrounded by cries of "Ça ira!" (It'll be fine!). (January 25, 1793)

off, blood spurts, the man is no more," Dr. Guillotin wrote proudly. The executioner then lifted the severed head by the hair and showed it to the spectators, to cheers of "Long live the Republic." For the first time in European history, a king met his end like a commoner.[36]

The Revolution grew even more violent after the king's death. (Marie Antoinette's head fell nine months after her husband's. Throughout her captivity she refused to give in to threats or confess to crimes she had not committed.) Rival groups had already formed in the National Convention, as always happens when large groups of people try to work together. One group called itself the Girondists, because its members came largely from the Gironde region of southwestern France. Girondists sat on the benches on the right side

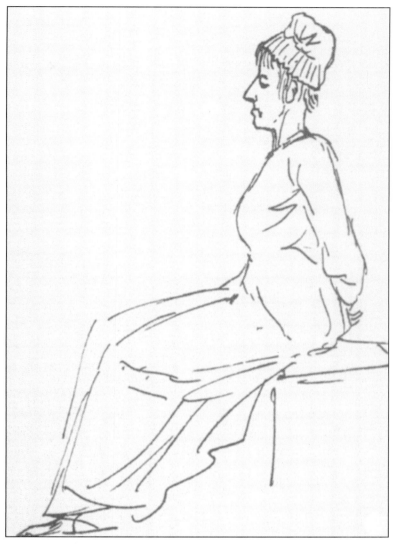

A drawing by Jacques-Louis David, who observed the scene from a nearby window, of a calm Marie Antoinette waiting to be beheaded. Her hair had been cut short to ensure a clean cut by the guillotine blade. (c. 1793)

of the meeting hall, which is the origin of the terms "the Right" and "right-wingers." Chiefly lawyers and prosperous businessmen, they favored property rights, wanting to limit the political power of the poor.

The Girondists' rivals, the Jacobins, took their name from their headquarters, a Paris monastery abandoned by the Jacobin monks. Chiefly lawyers, too, Jacobins wanted to give supreme power to the common people through their representatives—that is, themselves. Jacobins sat atop the "Mountain," the high benches on the left side of the meeting hall. We still call those with very liberal views "leftists" or "left-wingers." Most members of the National Convention, dubbed the "Plain," sat on the lower benches between the rival groups. Nowadays, we would call them "moderates" or "centrists."

The debate over the king's fate increased the rivals' bitterness. Historians note that revolutions, starting with the French Revolution, usually "devour their own"—destroy those who began them. Facing growing challenges and pressures, revolutionaries disagree over ideas, goals, and methods. Each group questions the other's loyalty to the cause. Tempers flare. Disagreements turn personal. Name-calling replaces discussion. Rivals are seen as not merely wrong, but evil. Harsh words lead to charges of treason, charges to arrests, and arrests to killing.

So it was by 1793. In June, the Jacobins led armed sansculottes in seizing power and forming a government under the National Convention's Committee of Public Safety. The committee's leader, thirty-five-year-old Maximilien de Robespierre, was a lawyer by profession and a fanatic by nature. A fussy little man, short and slim, he was often carried away by his feelings and beliefs. Robespierre worshiped the Revolution, to his mind humanity's greatest leap forward for liberty. In its defense, he said, "Liberty cannot be secured unless criminals lose their heads." By his definition, criminals were all who disagreed with him. Robespierre's colleagues (he had no friends) said he would happily guillo-

Maximilien de Robespierre, whose methods in the Reign of Terror would be closely studied by Joseph Stalin during the Red Terror in Russia 125 years later. (c. 1789–1795)

tine his own mother if he thought she might betray the sacred Revolution.[37]

To rid France of "traitors," Robespierre began the Reign of Terror, or simply the Terror. His creation left a poisonous legacy. "Terrorist" and "terrorism," now familiar terms, originated with the Reign of Terror. Robespierre's heirs were the twentieth century's mass murderers: Adolf Hitler in Germany, Mao Zedong in China, and Joseph Stalin in the Soviet Union. Stalin's secret police closely studied the Terror's methods, perfecting and applying them on a far larger scale.

"Terror," said Robespierre, "is nothing but prompt, severe, and inflexible justice." Thus, in the name of justice, the Terror ignored the Declaration of the Rights of Man and the Citizen. It became a law unto itself: judge, jury, and executioner. For starters, it sent scores of Girondists to the guillotine on trumped-up charges of treason.[38]

However, the Terror was not limited to the Jacobins' active opponents. Robespierre and his aides designed it to create such a climate of fear that nobody would dare think of resisting. The Terror spread like a cancer as local watch committees ordered all citizens to report "enemies of the people." Nobody was above suspicion. A wrong word overheard by the wrong person could cost you your life. Sellers of stale bread, butchers who raised prices, and soldiers who retreated went to the guillotine after a ten-minute trial, or no trial at all. Wig makers lost their heads because they catered to the nobility, making them "traitors in their hearts." So did former servants of the wealthy: butlers, maids, gardeners, and coachmen.

Entire families perished, not for anything they did, but for their ideas, politics, or social position. As she stood before the guillotine, Manon Roland, a Girondist, did not flinch. Slowly, with dignity, she bowed to the Statue of Liberty (the model for all others) standing across from the guillotine. "Oh, Liberty," she cried, "what crimes are committed in your name!" The poor woman realized that people may commit terrible crimes in the name of high-sounding ideals, but they are crimes nevertheless. In all, the Terror claimed about seventeen thousand victims in 1793.[39]

The Terror reached out for Thomas Paine, too. He was no longer France's hero; his pleas for mercy toward the king raised Jacobin suspicions that he was an English spy. On December 28, 1793, he wound up in an eight-by-ten-foot cell in the Luxembourg, a palace turned into a prison. We can only imagine Paine's thoughts as the door clanged behind him. For most

Manon Roland, a rare female political influencer, was sent to the guillotine after defecting from the Jacobins. (Date unknown)

prisoners, he knew, such a cell was the last stop before the guillotine.

Prison was the worst experience of Paine's life. "My friends," he wrote later, "were falling as fast as the guillotine could cut their heads off, and as I every day expected the same fate . . . I appeared to myself to be on my deathbed, for death was on every side of me." Each night, he heard guards dragging as many as fifty men and women from their cells and tossing them into carts bound for the "National Razor," slang for the guillotine. During one especially dreadful night, it claimed a record 169 inmates of the Luxembourg alone.[40]

The warden, an admirer of *Common Sense*, allowed its author to write to Gouverneur Morris, the U.S. ambassador to France. In 1787, as head of the Committee on Style and Arrangement, Morris gave the U.S. Constitution the form in which it exists today. Now, as ambassador, he had to look after the well-being of Americans in France. But he refused to ask for Paine's release. By sitting in the National Convention, Morris told Robespierre, Paine had declared himself a full French citizen, thus removing himself from American protection.[41]

After six months in prison, Paine fell ill. "My illness rendered me incapable of knowing anything that passed either in the prisons or elsewhere," he recalled. Since high fever made him unable to care for himself, guards moved him to a larger cell, where three fellow prisoners nursed him as best they could. Changing cells saved his life.[42]

On July 24, 1794, the end seemed near. It was a typical summer day in Paris, hot and muggy. To give him some fresh air, his cellmates got permission to keep the door open during the daylight hours. The door opened outward and rested flat against the corridor wall. That afternoon, the four men's names appeared on the death list. Guards passed each cell, chalking the number of condemned it held in red on each door. Come evening, a guard shut Paine's door without noticing that the number faced inside. At midnight, a fresh guard detail dragged screaming inmates from their cells, bypassing the unmarked door. Yet it was only a matter of time before other guards realized the error and corrected it.

Luckily for Paine, Robespierre had just accused leaders of the Plain of treason, a fatal error on his part. Rather than wait for arrest, they struck first. Despite a failed attempt to commit suicide in which he shattered his own jaw with a pistol shot, Robespierre went to the guillotine on July 28, and so did about a hundred of his aides. Robespierre howled with pain as the executioner ripped the bandages from his jaw before fastening the wooden collar on his neck. The Terror died with him. By then, it had claimed over twenty-six hundred lives in Paris and around sixteen thousand nationwide. Robespierre's fall opened the way for General Napoleon Bonaparte to "restore order" with a military dictatorship. Eventually, in May 1804, Napoleon crowned himself emperor of the French (meaning not only France, but *all* French people throughout the world).

Paine's fever broke a few days after Robespierre's fall. While Gouverneur Morris continued to refuse to

A cartoon showing Robespierre guillotining the executioner, after having guillotined everyone else in France. (Date unknown)

help, his replacement did not. James Monroe, later the fifth president of the United States, vouched for Paine's American citizenship. On November 6, 1794, after ten months and nine days, Paine walked through the gate of the Luxembourg, though still feeling himself a captive in France.

Paine spent more than a year as a guest in Monroe's Paris home while his body slowly healed. Yet the prison ordeal left him bitter, with a grudge against the man to whom he owed so much. George Washington remained a hero to the French. A word from the president would have been enough to set him free, Paine believed. Why, he wondered, had Washington left him to rot in that hellhole?

It is a fair question, but one historians cannot answer with certainty. We do know that Washington had serious concerns at this time. Eleven years after agreeing to American independence, England continued to hold on to various frontier forts. Moreover, each year the Royal Navy seized hundreds of American ships bound for France with trade goods. If Washington hoped to settle these issues, he dared not offend England. Helping Paine, whom its rulers despised, might have done just that, and even caused a war. Perhaps the president felt he could not take the risk. We would like to think so but will probably never know the truth.

Paine seethed with anger at Washington. Finally, it overflowed. In a public letter, dated July 30, 1796, he blasted the president. Paine accused the "father of our country" of having stolen the glory of better officers than he during the war, a reckless charge Paine could not prove. The president, he said, was a fraud, "treacherous in private friendship [and] a hypocrite in public life. The world will be puzzled to decide . . . whether

A portrait of James Monroe, who vouched for Paine's American citizenship, allowing him to leave prison in France. (c. 1914)

you have abandoned good principles, or whether you ever had any."[43]

The two men had once been friends. When signing his letters to Paine, Washington usually wrote, "Your sincere friend, G. Washington." Paine's letter infuriated him. It was, Washington told John Adams, the most insulting letter he had ever received. "[Paine] must have been insane to write so," Adams told his wife, Abigail.[44]

Those who knew Paine believed his incarceration had done something to his mind. For after leaving the Luxembourg, he attacked organized religion in his last great work, *The Age of Reason.*

CHAPTER 4

The Age of Reason

*It is by the exercise of our reason that we are
enabled to contemplate God and
His works, and imitate Him
in His ways.*

—Thomas Paine, "Of the Religion of Deism as
Compared with the Christian Religion," c. 1796

REVOLUTION AND RELIGION

In 1888, Theodore Roosevelt wrote a biography of Gouverneur Morris. The future twenty-sixth president was no ordinary politician. A dynamic, highly educated man, he had written several fine histories, including *The Naval War of 1812*. Now he called Thomas Paine a "filthy little atheist," literally "one without God," an unbeliever in the Almighty's existence. Roosevelt based this charge on *The Age of Reason,* which he may not have read, or read carefully enough to make such a harsh judgment. For Paine was no atheist— far from it. He believed in God from the bottom of his heart, but not as worshiped in churches or taught about in religious schools.[1]

Paine had wanted to write about religion for a long time. In 1776, soon after completing *Common Sense,* he visited John Adams. During their conversation, Adams recalled, the author expressed "contempt" for the Bible and "law-religions," his term for official state religions. "I have," Paine added, "some thoughts of publishing my Thoughts on Religion, but I believe it will be best to postpone it to the latter part of my life."[2]

He was ready to write it in 1793, driven by the need to save France from itself. Paine finished Part One of *The Age of Reason* in December, only hours before his

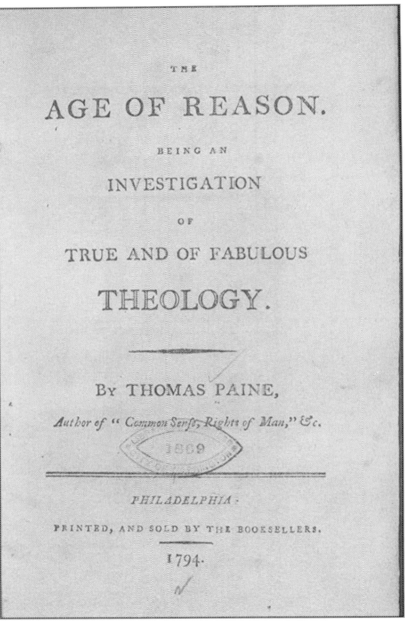

THE

AGE OF REASON.

BEING AN

INVESTIGATION

OF

TRUE AND OF FABULOUS

THEOLOGY.

By THOMAS PAINE,

Author of " Common Sense, Rights of Man," &c.

1869

PHILADELPHIA:

PRINTED, AND SOLD BY THE BOOKSELLERS.

1794.

The title page of The Age of Reason, *a portion of which Paine wrote while in prison.* (c. 1795)

arrest. Part Two, begun in prison, was completed in 1795 while Paine was recovering in the home of James Monroe.

Though Paine had welcomed the Revolution, he feared the results of its religious policies. Resentment of the church had continued to ferment. In July 1790, radicals in the National Assembly attacked the monarchy's ardent supporter and the nation's largest landowner. At their urging, the assembly ruled that, after a thousand years, France no longer had an official religion. Not only did the church lose its privileges, but all its money, property—lands, farms, parish churches, cathedrals, monasteries, nunneries, schools, hospitals—and other valuables went to the nation. The clergy, in turn, became paid civil servants, accountable to the state, and required to swear an oath of loyalty to it.

The loyalty oath posed a grave problem for the clergy. These men and women saw themselves as, above all, servants of God. Thus, taking the oath meant placing the state ahead of their sacred religious vows. Many, hoping to avoid trouble, took the oath anyway. In their minds, they remained faithful Catholics if they prayed, conducted religious services, and served their flocks. However, many other clergy, probably the majority, stood firm. Their consciences troubled, they refused to take the oath, in effect becoming criminals in the eyes of the government.

The National Assembly reacted forcefully, going all out to "dechristianize" France. It issued decrees closing all churches and ending religious services. Churches became stables and warehouses, their gold ornaments coined into money for paying the army. Armory workers melted church bells, using the bronze and iron to make guns. Vandals broke religious statues and monuments, smashing stained-glass windows and gravestones bearing the image of the cross. Bibles and prayer books ended up as shopkeepers' wrapping paper or toilet paper. Decrees abolished saints' days, feast days, and religious holidays. Priests, monks, and nuns had to marry. Those who objected (about twenty-five thousand) fled the country or went to the guillotine.

Opposition reached its peak in the Vendée, a region in western France bordering the Atlantic Ocean. For centuries, the Vendée had been staunchly Catholic, a place where the clergy served the people with devotion. It is no wonder, then, that persecuting them stirred resentment. Defying the government, protesters led by priests carried pictures of the Virgin Mary and sang hymns as they marched from village to village, farm to farm. Their opposition turned violent when Paris ordered thousands of young men drafted into the army.

A civil war within the Revolution began in March 1793, nine months before Paine's arrest. While both sides committed atrocities in the Vendée, government troops did the lion's share. As they poured into the region, soldiers turned it into a "sad desert" of ruined farms, burned crops, and leveled villages. "Wherever we pass by we bring flames and death," a captain wrote his sister. "What a war! We haven't seen a single individual without shooting them. Everywhere is strewn with corpses; everywhere the flames bring their ravages." When army units took many prisoners at once, they didn't know how to kill them fast enough. The guillotine was too slow. So was shooting, bayoneting, and burning them in barns or churches. The solution lay in so-called "patriotic baptisms," tying scores of rebels and priests together and drowning them in rivers.[3]

THE CHALLENGE

Everywhere Paine turned, France seemed as if it was "running headlong into atheism." The Revolution, he felt, was losing its moral character. As sure as night follows day, he saw the attack on Christianity leading to atheism, and finally to the collapse of all human values. Left without a guide to right and wrong, France, he feared, would see the end of morality and decency, love and pity.

Paine blamed the looming disaster not just on fanatical politicians but also on Christianity. Like all organized religions, he argued, it rested on myths, not reason. Supposedly devised by corrupt priests, it aimed at controlling people's minds so the ruling classes might easily exploit them. Thus, Paine wrote *The Age of Reason* to fight atheism by replacing organized religion with the "true religion of nature."[4]

His ideas were hardly original. They had been around for well over a century. Though formally still Christians, members of the European and American elite were often Deists, from the Latin *deus,* or "God." Deists were simply believers in God.

Also called the religion of reason, Deism had its roots in history and science. History is filled with examples of established state religions using their power to persecute. In the Middle Ages, European Catholics launched Crusades, or "wars of the Cross," to conquer Muslim lands in the Middle East. Muslims, in turn, waged holy wars, called jihads, or "struggles in the way of God." During jihads, they demanded that conquered Christians convert to Islam. Those who refused had to pay a tax; those who would not pay were killed. Later, millions of European Catholics and Protestants died in

Anneken Hendriks, an Anabaptist accused of heresy, being burned alive in Amsterdam in 1571. (c. 1685)

A cartoon by George
Cruikshank showing a
"freeborn Englishman"
standing on the Bill of Rights
and the Magna Carta. In
his pinioned hand he holds a
note that reads, "Freedom of
the Press—Transportation,"
meaning transportation
to Australia as a convict.
(c. 1819)

the Thirty Years' War (1618–1648). In Germany in the 1640s, one might ride in the countryside for days without seeing a living soul. Meanwhile, in Russia, members of the Orthodox Church murdered hundreds of thousands of Jews.

Questioning the official state religion was dangerous. Until its abolition in the early 1800s, the Spanish Inquisition tortured and burned heretics, those holding beliefs different from the Catholic Church's. "In most countries in Europe," John Adams wrote Thomas Jefferson, "[heresy] is punished by fire at the stake, or the rack, or the wheel. In England itself it is punished by boring through the tongue with a red-hot poker." James Madison agreed. "Religious bondage," the future fourth president wrote, "shackles and debilitates the mind and unfits it for every noble enterprise." "Enlightened" people disgustedly rejected traditional churches.[5]

Sir Isaac Newton was the second source

of Deism. The scientist, we recall, had shown that everything in the universe acts according to precise mathematical laws. Newton's discovery changed how some thought about God. Deists compared the universe to a watch. They believed that after creating it, God, the "Divine Watchmaker," wound it up—that is, set in motion its governing laws. His work done, God stepped aside, leaving the "watch" to run by itself forever, perfectly and un-

A portrait of Sir Isaac Newton, a major influence upon Deism. (c. 1760)

changingly. Deists used various names for the Almighty: Providence, First Cause, Supreme Being, Creator of the Universe, and the Grand Architect. Our Declaration of Independence speaks of "the Laws of Nature and Nature's God."

Deists held that organized religions failed the test of reason. Religious truth, they said, comes not from holy books or revelation, God's speaking directly to favored individuals. It comes from the very existence of the world. According to Deists, God gave humans reason, the ability to observe nature and think logically about it. As Paine wrote in an undated essay, "In Deism our reason and our belief become happily united. The wonderful structure of the universe, and everything we behold in the system of the creation, prove to us, far better than books can do, the existence of God."[6]

It followed that to admire the creation is to worship the Creator. We honor God, Deists claimed, by serving our fellow man. Benjamin Franklin put it best: "Serving God is doing good to man." Franklin, who described himself in his *Autobiography* as "a thorough Deist," thought oppressing anyone for their religious beliefs the worst form of stupidity and savagery.[7]

Other Founding Fathers were Deists, too. In 1831, Dr. Bird Wilson, a respected Protestant minister, interviewed people who had known the Founders. Nearly all, Wilson discovered, had been Deists. As for George Washington, "he was a Deist and nothing more." In answer to Wilson's questions about the first president's faith, his own pastor declared, "Sir, Washington was a Deist." Washington seldom used the word "God," preferring terms like "Almighty Being" or "Invisible Hand."[8]

Thomas Jefferson, politician and amateur scientist, saw the hand of God in nature. Though a slave owner who broke up families for sale when short of cash, he despised cruelty in the name of God. Jefferson damned "priestcraft," his term for what he saw as the clergy's lust for power and wealth. Moreover, he argued that when church and state unite, they always harm the people. That is why the U.S. Constitution guarantees religious freedom, building what Jefferson called "a wall of separation between church and state." In America, churches have no right to meddle in government affairs, and government has no right to dictate what churches should or should not teach.[9]

In his *Notes on the State of Virginia* (1785), Jefferson wrote: "Millions of innocent men, women, and children, since the introduction of Christianity, have been burnt, tortured, fined, imprisoned [for their beliefs]. . . . What has been the effect of coercion? To make one half of the world fools, and the other half hypocrites." Nevertheless, he admired Jesus Christ as an enlightened reformer, whose teachings, he said, priests twisted with "hocus-pocus" and "abracadabra." To learn the truth as Jesus taught it, Jefferson took scissors and paste to the Bible, cutting out "true" passages and trashing the rest. He called his version of the Bible *The Life and Morals of Jesus of Nazareth.*[10]

The title page of The Life and Morals of Jesus of Nazareth, *now commonly known as* The Jefferson Bible. *(c. 1820)*

Thomas Paine echoed the Deists' beliefs. Part One of *The Age of Reason* is a blistering attack on organized religion, and Christianity in particular. He began by stating his personal faith in the clearest terms possible.

I believe in one God, and no more; and I hope for happiness beyond this life.

*I believe [in] the equality of man, and I
believe that religious duties consist in doing justice,
loving mercy, and endeavoring to make our
fellow-creatures happy.*

*But lest it should be supposed that I believe many
other things in addition to these, I shall . . . declare
the things I do not believe, and my reasons for not
believing them.*

*I do not believe in the creed professed by the
Jewish church, by the Roman [Catholic] church,
by the Greek [Orthodox] church, by the Turkish
[Muslim] church, by the Protestant church, nor by
any church that I know of. My own mind is my own
church.*

*All [official state] churches . . . appear to me to
be no other than human inventions set up to terrify
and enslave mankind, and monopolize power and
profit. . . .*

*Each of those churches shows certain books, which
they call* revelation, *or the Word of God. The Jews say
that their Word of God was given by God to Moses,
face to face; the Christians say that their Word of
God came by divine inspiration; and the [Muslims]
say that their word of God (the Koran) was brought
by an angel from heaven. Each of those churches
accuses the other of unbelief; and, for my part,
I disbelieve them all.*[11]

Part Two is a book-by-book, chapter-and-verse attack on the Bible, both the Old and New Testaments. Paine had nothing good to say about the holy scriptures of Judaism and Christianity. He called the Bible "this pretended Word of God," a human invention "written by priests." It was "a book of lies, wickedness and blasphemy" that had "served to corrupt and brutalize mankind." Paine ended by denouncing "this thing called Christianity" as "too absurd for belief," a fraud that "produces only atheists and fanatics." To know God, he wrote, is to know that "the Creator of man is the Creator of science, and it is through that medium that man can see God, as it were, face to face," and "not the stupid texts of the Bible."[12]

FIGHTING WORDS

Even those who had once praised the author as a champion of liberty thought *The Age of Reason* foolish, bigoted, and unfair. In Paine's zeal to attack genuine abuses, he had gone too far.

To claim that Christianity had never done any good was to ignore history. Through the ages, Christianity satisfied basic human needs, such as coping with the loss of loved ones. It inspired music, art, and literature that allowed even the humblest to lead richer lives. It also saved countless lives. In Roman times, for example, the Catholic Church banned the gruesome "games" in which gladiators fought to the death to amuse audiences. Later, it took in unwanted children, rather than allow poor parents to abandon them, as was the custom. Church-run schools taught millions of children to read and write. In Paine's America, a Protestant religious revival in the early 1800s aimed at getting the nation "right with God" by fighting social evils. Religious people denounced gambling, whiskey drinking, and cruelty to animals. Above all, they campaigned to abolish slavery.

What most offended Paine's critics was not so much *what* he said, but *how* he said it and to *whom*. As with *Common Sense* and *Rights of Man,* he wrote for the masses. Before they could act on a problem, Paine knew, he first had to make them think about it. And that meant grabbing their attention with the printed word.

Paine once described his method to an American friend. "It is necessary to be bold," he said. "Some people can be reasoned into sense, and others must be shocked into it. Say a bold thing that will stagger them, and they will begin to think." Naturally, critics—particularly clergymen—resented his strong language. Worse, by mocking the Bible, and making Deism understandable to the uneducated, Paine seemed to be preaching atheism, though he meant to do the exact opposite.[13]

Until *The Age of Reason* appeared, Deism had been a faith for the elite, dressed up in learned language in expensive books. The elite never broadcast their beliefs, or dreamed of shocking common folk. Besides, talking openly about Deism would have upset traditional believers, ending politicians' careers. In 1757, for example, an unidentified writer asked Benjamin Franklin's opinion of his essay on Deism. The old man's answer could have applied to Paine thirty-five years later. Franklin warned that publishing the essay would cause no end "of mischief to you," adding, "He that spits against the Wind, spits in his own Face." Therefore, Franklin said, "I would advise you . . . to burn this Piece before it is seen by any other Person, whereby you will save yourself a great deal of [sorrow] by the Enemies it may raise against you."[14]

Paine spat into the wind. Since the appearance of

Rights of Man, England's rulers had gone wild at the very sound of his name. That book had given commoners the ideas and words to challenge the system of government. Now Paine's latest work threatened to arouse them further, destroying faith in God and morality. If commoners read things like *The Age of Reason*, some asked, why teach reading at all? "Giving education to the laboring classes or the poor," a judge observed, "would teach them to despise their lot in life. . . . Instead of teaching them subordination, it would render them fractious [restless] and refractory [unruly]." American slave owners applied the same logic to their human "property." For that reason, Southern states had laws banning the teaching of slaves to read and write.[15]

In London, the government ordered another crackdown. As with *Rights of Man*, its book police went after printers and sellers of *The Age of Reason*. All copies they seized went into the fire. Cartoonists drew vile pictures with titles like "THE AGE OF REASON: or the World turned topsy-turvy exemplified in Tom Paine's WORKS!!" This cartoon showed, among other outrages, the author plunging a spear into the crucified Christ.

Paine could afford to ignore the uproar in England; its government could not touch him in France. By the late 1790s, however, he had given up on France. His friend-turned-enemy Edmund Burke had been right to point out the Revolution's dark side, though Paine would never give him credit for doing so. Fanaticism had betrayed its own professed ideals. Instead of *Liberté, Égalité, Fraternité,* Robespierre and his crew

Another cartoon by George Cruikshank, this one depicting a world "turned topsy-turvy" by Paine and his ideas. (c. 1819)

had created bloody chaos. In 1799, General Napoleon Bonaparte seized control of the government, in effect bringing the Revolution to an end. Five years later, he crowned himself emperor of the French. To win popular support, he ended the fighting in the Vendée, reopened the churches, and allowed priests and nuns to return from exile. Yet the emperor, cynical and ambitious to the core, would give Europe another decade of war. We call it the era of the Napoleonic Wars.

"This is not a country for an honest man to live in," Paine groaned. The French "do not understand anything at all of the principles of free government, and the best way is to leave them to themselves." As for Napoleon, at first the author had seen him as a force for stability. However, after 1804, Paine read him perfectly. Napoleon was "the completest charlatan that ever existed . . . willful, headstrong, proud, morose. Tyrants in general shed blood upon plan or from passion; he seems to have shed it only because he could not be quiet."[16]

Paine wanted to go home, to America In 1800, President-elect Jefferson urged him to return. Though he longed to leave France, he dared not. France and England were at war. Branded an outlaw by England, he feared for his life should he fall into English hands. If he sailed, even aboard an American ship, an English man-of-war might easily stop it, search it, and clap him in chains. Luckily, Napoleon agreed to a brief truce with the island nation, allowing him to sail in safety. On October 30, 1802, his ship docked at Baltimore, Maryland. Paine was sixty-five years old and had been away fifteen years. He had no idea that *The Age of Reason* had made him a marked man in America, and that the uproar over it would poison his old age.

CHAPTER 5

An Honest and Useful Life

I have lived an honest and useful life to mankind;
my time has been spent in doing good.

—Thomas Paine, "Last Will and Testament,"
January 18, 1809

THE YOUNG REPUBLIC

During his years in Europe, Paine had followed events in America as best he could in the newspapers. When delegates to the Constitutional Convention approved the U.S. Constitution in September 1787, he saluted their wisdom and patriotism. It was vital, he wrote, to place thirteen separate, and often feuding, states under a central government, forming a truly United States of America. "United, she is formidable," Paine wrote, "separated, she is a medley of individual nothings, subject to the sport of foreign nations." He also praised the Bill of Rights, the first ten amendments to the Constitution. These guaranteed the civil liberties he'd always called for in his writings: freedom of religion, speech, and the press and a fair trial for anyone charged with a crime.[1]

Meanwhile, men who had worked together to get their states to ratify the Constitution began quarreling over government policies. From their quarrels grew the nation's first political parties, the Federalist and the Democratic-Republican, or Republican for short. The rise of parties troubled Paine, as it did others who feared a repeat of the political corruption eating away at England. These people saw parties as cliques and cabals, groups pursuing their selfish interests while pretending to work for the common good. Yet, like it or not, parties were to play a key role in American political life. No history of our country is complete without considering the role they have played over the centuries.

Ideas about the scope and role of government divided the parties, as they still do. Each party represented different interests and drew support from different areas of the country—again, as they still do.

The Federalists, strongest in New England, championed the well-to-do, for the nation could not prosper without their investments and ingenuity. Federalists demanded, for example, high taxes on imported goods to protect growing, or "infant," industries from foreign competition.

It followed that the young republic needed the stability only a strong federal government could give. According to the Constitution, this means that the states have certain powers. These include control of their police, courts, education, voting rights, and taxation for

John Adams beat Thomas Jefferson to become the second president of the United States. (Date unknown)

state needs. Other, greater powers are reserved for the federal government. Among these is the power to tax all citizens, regulate trade between states, conduct diplomacy with foreign nations, and raise a national military force. Federalists believed in enforcing federal powers to the fullest. In this way, government would protect private property, promote prosperity, and keep the "common Herd of Mankind" (Burke's "swinish multitude") in line. The ignorant, the poor, and those without property, Federalists insisted, must never get a chance to start a French-style revolution, butchering the "better sort."[2]

John Adams, the leading Federalist, was a grumpy little man with a ferocious temper, a quick mind, and a sharp tongue. Adams's knowledge of history led him to distrust democracy. Like Edmund Burke, he believed that "all men are bad by their nature"—vain, jealous, greedy, violent. "Remember, democracy never lasts long," he wrote. "It soon wastes, exhausts, and murders itself. There never was a democracy that did not commit suicide." So it had been with the city-states of ancient Greece and the Roman Republic in Julius Caesar's time. It is no accident that "tyrant" comes from the Greek *tyrannos,* an absolute ruler bound by no law; "dictator," from the Latin *dictatus,* means much the same. Would history repeat itself in America?[3]

Thomas Jefferson, the Republican leader, hoped not. Based mostly in the South and West, his party drew support from ranchers, farmers, and plantation owners. In the mid-Atlantic states, Republicans appealed to small-time merchants, urban laborers, and recent immigrants. Such people saw a too-powerful federal government and military as threats to civil liberties. Republicans also opposed high import taxes because they raised consumer prices on manufactured goods.

Jefferson had no use for kings and nobles immoral fools who fought wars with other people's blood. He also despised "moneymen"—bankers and stock traders—who made fortunes by managing money while producing nothing. Unlike John Adams, Jefferson trusted the common people, their good sense and basic decency. Thus, for him, "the will of the majority is the only sure guardian of the rights of men." Jefferson's ideal America had neither rich nor poor, but was a place where all had enough to live in modest comfort—all, that is, but enslaved blacks. (Jefferson, we note, had several children with his slave Sally Hemings.) To keep the federal government responsive to the people, he wished to limit its power in favor of increased self-rule by states and local communities.[4]

Federalists and Republicans disagreed on the French Revolution, too. Stunned by the Terror, fearing "infection by French principles," Federalists saw England as the only real check on French aggression. Despite all the violence, however, Republicans continued to believe that France stood for liberty—that, in the end, its principles would overcome the current madness. In Philadelphia, theater bands struck up "Ça ira" as audiences bellowed the rallying song of the Paris mobs. When it came to the Revolution, even the mild-mannered Jefferson showed a callous, brutal streak unworthy of him. While he regretted the loss of innocent lives, Jefferson still defended the Revolution. "Rather than it should have failed," he wrote, "I would have seen half the earth desolated. Were there but an Adam & an Eve left in every country, & left free" to restart the human race, he thought the cost worthwhile. He never seemed to consider how the unlucky victims might have felt.[5]

With the help of George Washington, a Federalist ally but not a party member, John Adams won the presidential election of 1796. This horrified Paine because, he growled, "John Adams has such a talent for blundering and offending." The feeling was mutual. While Adams credited Paine with turning colonists' minds toward independence in 1776, he detested the author, calling him "too democratical," too trusting in the common people.[6]

While England and France seized American merchant ships bound for each other's ports, Federalists were angriest with France. Thanks to President Adams, the navy built several first-rate warships, including the *Constitution*. Nicknamed "Old Ironsides" because cannon-balls bounced off her oak sides, she launched in 1797 during an undeclared sea war with France. Often American ships had running gun battles with French men-of-war. Meanwhile, the Federalist-dominated Congress passed, at Adams's urging, the Alien and Sedition Acts. These allowed the government to deport any foreign-born person it thought "dangerous" and made it a crime to criticize the government. Apparently, for Federalists, the Bill of Rights did not apply in national emergencies.

Thomas Jefferson became the third president of the United States after one of the most polarizing elections in the history of the country. (c. 1898)

Jefferson defeated Adams in the election of 1800. Never before or since has the nation seen such a shameful, insult-filled contest. Each side went after the other as if it were pure evil. Federalists branded Jefferson a "half-injun, half-negro," a "howling atheist," and a vulgar rabble-rouser. In Sunday sermons, ministers declared that, if elected, Jefferson would force Christians to hide their family Bibles and pray in secret, as in France. Jefferson's supporters hit back, charging Adams with being a toothless old man and "quite mad." Why, he even had a secret plan to crown himself king![7]

Thousands of voters were recent immigrants, mostly English and Irish, who took their political ideas from *Rights of Man*. When they arrived, they found Federalists in control. As in their home countries, they accused the ruling party of selfishly increasing the powers of government. The federal administration had become, they said, a meddling tyrant, determined "to have a finger in every pie." They thought taxes were sky-high and the money was badly spent, claims that have echoed throughout American history. In reply, they formed political clubs and started newspapers that helped swing the election to Jefferson.[8]

Attitudes toward Paine mirrored the political conflict. When he returned, Republicans welcomed "the People's Friend" home. Federalists, however, wished to punish him for insulting George Washington and writing *The Age of Reason,* which offended most Americans' religious beliefs. Old friends who had once hailed his patriotism would have nothing to do with him now. For example, Samuel Adams, John's cousin, had helped organize the Boston Tea Party. During the War for Independence, he and Paine became close friends. Not anymore. "Do you think," Adams asked, "that your pen . . . can unchristianize the mass of our citizens, or have you hopes of converting a few of them to assist you in so bad a cause?" Paine's book literally made devout Federalists sick to their stomachs.[9]

Without meaning to, Paine gave Jefferson's political enemies a weapon—himself. Attacking the author became a way of hammering the president as well. Federalist newspapers damned Paine as a "lying, drunken, brutal infidel," though he wrote to combat atheism and opposed the Terror. Federalist posters showed horned demons dragging the author into the fires of hell. Some bore poems like this gem, printed in bold black letters:

The Fox has lost his Tail
The Ass has done his Braying
The Devil has got Tom Paine.[10]

Though no Deist, John Adams thought the Bible contained "whole cartloads of trumpery." Nevertheless, he went to church regularly, believing Christianity had done humanity far more good than harm. *The Age of Reason,* he insisted, was doing far more harm than good. Adams scorned its author, none too delicately, as "a mongrel between a Pigg and Puppy, begotten by a wild Boar on a Bitch Wolf." As for Jefferson, Federalists relished the thought of his slaves using Paine's bloody remains as manure to fertilize crops at Monticello, his Virginia plantation. Paine hit back. Calling Federalists "witless curs," he accused them of wishing to slaughter Americans in a new Reign of Terror. Like the charges against him, this was nonsense. But the insults show how hatred can carry away normally sensible people.[11]

To show his support, Jefferson often invited Paine to the unfinished White House, then the largest house in the country. In 1800, the nation's capital was set in what Abigail Adams called "a romantic but a wild

An illustration of the White House in 1807.

An illustration of the White House in 1807.

wilderness." Approaching Washington, D.C., by coach, she found "nothing but a Forest & woods on the way, for 16 and 18 miles not a village. Here and there a thatched cottage without a single pane of glass, inhabited by Blacks." The city had a population of 291, including 152 members of Congress. Croaking bullfrogs kept them up at night while swarms of mosquitoes rose from swamps along the Potomac River to torment them. Cows grazed on the National Mall amid thousands of tree stumps and stagnant pools of water. A visitor could hardly believe the number of "dead cats and all kinds of putridity" floating in drainage ditches near the White House.[12]

Nobody could miss the gangs of stonecutters, bricklayers, and carpenters working on the Capitol and other government buildings. All were enslaved black people; the government rented them from their owners for about a dollar a day, plus food. Paine must have seen these gangs but did not mention them in his writings—at least in those that have survived. Congressmen saw "the two Toms" arm in arm, strolling in the evening cool. "Our stomachs," a Federalist newspaper groaned, "nauseate at the sight of their affectionate embrace."[13]

War clouds were gathering as they strolled. Recently, Napoleon had forced Spain to give France the Louisiana Territory, an 828,000-square-mile tract of land between the Mississippi River and the Rocky Mountains. Before withdrawing its forces, Spain had closed the port of New Orleans to American shipping, and Napoleon continued the policy. Frontier communities as far as a thousand miles upriver relied on the Mississippi to take their products—wheat, hogs, cattle, and timber—to New Orleans and, from there, to European markets.

Federalists reacted to the shutdown by urging war with France. Paine, however, had a better idea. He told the president that Napoleon was starved for money to finance his wars. So why not offer to buy the entire Louisiana Territory? Jefferson thanked him for the suggestion, adding that he had already decided to do just that. He made an offer Napoleon could not refuse. On May 3, 1803, the United States paid the bargain price of $15 million, or three cents an acre. Jefferson had doubled the size of his country with the stroke of a pen; the nation now stretched from the Atlantic to the Rockies. The following spring, Jefferson sent army officers Meriwether Lewis and William Clark on their epic journey to explore the western lands.

Thomas Paine's cottage in New Rochelle, New York. (c. 1875–1907)

GROWING OLD

Sadness filled Paine's last years. With advancing age, he spent the cold months in various New York City boardinghouses, the warm months in his New Rochelle cottage. His possessions there included a rickety table and chairs, a musty feather bed, a few cracked dishes, a teapot, and some silverware. From time to time, an unidentified free black woman cooked his meals; he favored buckwheat cakes drowned in melted butter.

Paine had always drunk more alcohol than he should have. An Irish friend reported from Paris: "He drinks brandy in such profusion, as to reduce him nearly to a state of insensibility." Another put it more simply: "He drinks like a fish." Now more often drunk than sober, Paine downed a quart of brandy every day. He drank to forget his loneliness and dull the aches and pains of aging. Until painkillers such as aspirin became available in the early twentieth century, alcohol made life easier—at least if consumed in moderation.[14]

The more Paine drank, the more he neglected himself. He grew seedier, sloppier, and smellier. William Carver, a blacksmith Paine knew, once came to visit him. Finding the cottage empty, Carver searched all around New Rochelle. Finally, he found Paine in a tavern. After Paine sobered up, Carver scolded him for not shaving for two weeks. His shirt was in tatters, "nearly the color of tanned leather, and you had the most disagreeable smell possible, just like that of the poor beggars in England. Do you recollect the pains I took to clean you? That I got a tub of warm water and soap, and washed you from head to foot, and this I had to do three times, before I could get you clean. I likewise shaved you and cut your nails, that were like birds' claws. . . . Many of your toenails exceeded half an inch in length, and others had grown round your toes."[15]

When not drunk, Paine sat at his table for hours, lost in despair. Of course, the insults, unfair criticism, and name-calling hurt. But he could take these in stride, as part of the rough-and-tumble of politics. At least American politicians did not send rivals to the guillotine! What hurt most was the realization that he had returned to a changed and strange America—an America that had passed him by.

As we grow old, it is said, we stay the same (at least to ourselves), while the world changes around us. Everything changes with time. New generations have new ideas, new interests, and new challenges. So it was with Paine's America. The generation that had grown up since independence seemed to know little, and care less, about their elders' sacrifices. The spirit of '76, the hot idealism of "the times that tried men's souls," had cooled. America was fast becoming a land of undreamed-of opportunity. Countless young people thought only of buying and selling, making money and getting ahead; they called themselves go-aheads. Their motto was:

> *On others inspiration flash,*
> *Give them eternal fame—*
> *But give me cash!*[16]

Other aging revolutionaries shared Paine's despair. Among them was Benjamin Rush, who had inspired him to write *Common Sense*. A signer of the Declaration of Independence, Rush "felt like a stranger" in the land of his birth. Worship of the almighty dollar had replaced the ideals of the Founders. America had grown hideous in Rush's eyes, "a bewhiskered and a bedollared nation."[17]

George Washington came to doubt Americans' capacity for self-government. By putting party above country, he wrote in 1799, shortly before his death, politicians had made theirs a low, grubby profession, no career for decent folks. Federalists and Republicans could, he noted grimly, "set up a broomstick" as a candidate and "it will command [party loyalists'] votes in toto."[18]

Thomas Jefferson, the fervent democrat, came to dread the future of American democracy. In January 1825, the ex-president wrote in despair of the Founders' generation: "All, all dead, and ourselves alone amidst a new generation whom we know not, and who knows not us." All the patriots' suffering and sacrifice—what had they accomplished?[19]

John Adams agreed with his former opponent. "I am buried and forgotten," he moaned. Rather than shaping a better world, he saw the years after independence as an "age of Folly, Vice, Frenzy, Fury, [Demons], Brutality." Yet as time would tell, the old-timers had been too pessimistic. For the spirit of '76 lived alongside the changes they despised. (Adams and Jefferson died on the same day, July 4, 1826, the fiftieth anniversary of the signing of the Declaration of Independence.)[20]

Meanwhile, Thomas Paine went downhill. In July 1806, as the emperor Napoleon became virtual master of Europe, Paine had a stroke. "The fit took me on the stairs," the author reported, "as suddenly as if I had been shot through the head." He was never the same. Paine was bedridden, his body covered by pus-filled sores caused by lying too long in the same position. He could barely keep food down; nearly everything he ate or drank, including brandy, caused vomiting.[21]

Uninvited visitors became an ordeal. After learning that the author of *The Age of Reason* had rented a room in the Greenwich Village section of New York, local ministers came calling. Haughty men, proud of their wisdom and virtue, they looked down on the ailing revolutionary. Paine must, they insisted, renounce his "atheistical" work and get "right" with God by embracing Christianity. Enough! Paine sent them away, and not with gentle words.

Another time, an elderly woman barged into his room.

"What do you want?" said Paine, trapped in bed.

"Is your name Paine?"

"Yes."

"Well, then, I come from Almighty God, to tell you that if you do not repent of your sins and believe in our blessed Savior Jesus Christ, you will be damned and—"

Paine cut her off. "Pooh, pooh, it is not true," he cried, his voice crackling with anger. "[Jesus] would not send such a foolish ugly old woman as you . . . with His message. Go away. Go away. Shut the door." Shocked, she left without another word.[22]

Feeling his life ebbing away, Paine put his affairs in order. In January 1809, he wrote his will. After leaving his possessions to friends, he made his final declaration of faith. A Deist to the end, he wrote: "I die in perfect composure and resignation to the will of my Creator, God."[23]

At eight o'clock on the morning of June 8, 1809, Paine died in his sleep, in his seventy-third year. He had wanted to be buried in a Quaker graveyard in New York, but they would not have

The Greenwich Village house on Bleecker Street where Thomas Paine spent his last few years. (c. 1914)

the author of *The Age of Reason*. So he left instructions to bury him in a corner of a field on his New Rochelle farm.

When Benjamin Franklin died in 1790, more than twenty thousand mourners came to the funeral. During Paine's lifetime, he had known hundreds of important people in the United States, England, and France. Not one of them, including Thomas Jefferson, publicly mentioned his passing. Only five attended the funeral: Marguerite de Bonneville, a French refugee who had cared for him from time to time, her son Benjamin, a friend named Willett Hicks, and "two negroes."[24]

The mourners gathered around the open grave. As falling earth thump-thumped on the coffin, Mrs. Bonneville spoke. "Oh! Mr. Paine!" she said with emotion. "My son stands here as testimony of the gratitude of America, and I, for France!"[25]

A week later, unnamed friends put up a simple headstone. As he had directed in his will, it read: "Thomas Paine, Author of 'Common Sense.' "[26]

PAINE FOR A NEW AGE

During the following years, New Rochelle's children made up a song about the man buried in the field by the road:

> *Poor Tom Paine! There he lies,*
> *Nobody laughs and nobody cries.*
> *Where he has gone and how he fares,*
> *Nobody knows and nobody cares.*

They were wrong. Many still cared about Paine and his ideas.[27]

Paine died when England was quickly becoming the "workshop of the world." The Industrial Revolution was in full swing, as producers began using novel types of machinery to manufacture their goods. Originally, the word "manufacture" meant to make an object by hand; *manus* is Latin for "hand." That changed with the invention of steam-powered machinery in the 1760s. By gathering many machines in one place, called a factory, more things could be made more cheaply than ever before.

Think of clothing. Until the Industrial Revolution, most Europeans could afford only one set of woolen garments, worn in all seasons, and often no linen underwear at all. Unable to change into fresh clothes, they wore these garments to shreds before replacing them. By the time Paine died, the Southern states had begun to specialize in slave-grown cotton, an inexpensive fiber easy to wash. Since even most poor people could afford cotton garments and a few sets of underwear, they could easily wash the dirty while changing into the clean. In this way, they lived longer by avoiding diseases like lice-borne typhus. Since they also itched less, they scratched less and had fewer skin infections. They smelled better, too.

But progress also brought hardship. To cut operating costs and increase profits, factory owners demanded that workers put in longer hours at lower wages. To cut costs further, they hired children at a fraction of an adult's wages. Most of these children's parents could not afford to feed them or send them to school; other children were orphans. Owners rented them from orphanages at a few pence a day per "head." Children as young as five toiled fifteen-hour days in textile factories, coal mines, and steel mills. Each year, hundreds met with accidents. In English cotton mills, for example, overworked, overtired children might get careless. A false move might result in their being pulled into the gears of a machine, crippling or killing them.

Adult workers formed unions to demand better conditions and laws banning child labor. Employers often resisted such demands, denouncing unions as "Jacobin" clubs and their leaders as "little Robespierres." To enforce their demands, unions went on strike. Called "war by another name," strikes might last for months, bringing entire towns to the verge of starvation. Desperate to feed their families, strikers chanted slogans such as:

Peace and large bread
Or a king without a head.[28]

When strikes turned into violent "bread or blood" riots, army officers, as usual, read the Riot Act before their redcoats opened fire. Judges sentenced captured rioters to prison, the gallows, or forced labor in Australia.[29]

English workers took inspiration from Thomas Paine's writings. Despite every effort by the book

Two young boys working in a factory comfort one another.
(c. 1840)

police, Paine's words continued to lead a secret life. Groups of "Painites" met at night in cellars to read, by candlelight, and discuss precious copies of *Rights of Man* and *The Age of Reason*. In this way, Paine's ideas influenced many who had not thought in those terms before.[30]

In 1819, William Cobbett, an English journalist who wrote under the name Peter Porcupine, dug up Paine's body and took it back to his native land. "He belongs to England," the grave robber declared. "His fame is the property of England." Cobbett planned to put the body on display, charging visitors to see it. He would then use the money to build a monument to Paine that, he hoped, would become a rallying point for reformers. When nothing came of the project, Cobbett stored the body in, of all places, a box under his bed! Upon Cobbett's death, the box passed from person to person for several years. One owner wrote his name on Paine's skull. Another cracked it open for a souvenir: "I took a portion of his brain, which has become hard, and is almost black." Eventually, box, brain, and bones vanished. By now, they have probably turned to dust.[31]

Over the years, Paine became a hero to English working people. Jailed for striking, they hung crude drawings of him, mass-produced on illegal printing presses, on their cell walls. Union meetings often began with a rousing song, set to the tune of "God Save the King," the national anthem (when a king is sovereign).

> *God Save Great Thomas Paine*
> *His* Rights of Man *explain*
> *To every soul.*

He makes the blind to see
What dupes and slaves they be,
And points out liberty
From pole to pole.[32]

When, in 1867, Parliament gave men (but not women) the right to vote regardless of their income, part of the credit for this "peaceful revolution" went to Paine. The union-based Labor Party, formed in the early 1900s, continued to honor him. In 1964, Cobbett's monument became a reality. In Thetford, a bronze statue depicts the author holding a pen in his right hand and *Rights of Man* in his left. This and other writings are now available, free of charge, on various Internet sites. There is also a Thomas Paine Society, whose mission is to inspire citizens to action through transmission of his ideas.

LEGACY

As it turned out, America had not lost the spirit of '76 after all. Paine's writings continued to influence reformers. In a society dominated by men, these writings energized early champions of women's rights. During the 1830s, Fanny Wright, the "female Thomas Paine," demanded equality in words that could have come from *Rights of Man*. Elizabeth Cady Stanton and Lucretia Mott admired Paine and built on Wright's work. In 1848, they organized the nation's first women's rights convention at Seneca Falls, New York. Undoubtedly influenced by *Common Sense,* Stanton won the convention's approval for a Declaration of Sentiments, which she modeled on the Declaration of Independence. But

A caricature of Fanny Wright, the equality activist known as "the female Thomas Paine." The caption's reference to Wright as a "gabbler" probably alludes to her sensational lecture tour of 1829. (c. 1829)

A DOWNRIGHT GABBLER, or a goose that deserves to be hissed_

A postage stamp, issued in 1969, paying tribute to Thomas Paine.

instead of saying "all men are created equal," Stanton wrote "all men and women are created equal."[33]

Like their English cousins, American workers took inspiration from Paine's writings. In the 1830s, unions in New York, Boston, and other cities honored his memory with annual birthday dances and celebrations. At union rallies in the early 1900s, speakers celebrated *The Age of Reason* as "a work containing more truth than any volume under the Sun." When inducting members, union officials often handed out paperback editions of *Rights of Man* with their membership cards. In 1969, the U.S. Postal Service issued a forty-cent stamp in tribute to Paine. Today, Washington, D.C., plans to build a Paine memorial on the National Mall.[34]

Union leader Eugene V. Debs, five-time candidate for president, hero-worshiped Paine. "The revolutionary history of the United States and France stirred me deeply and its heroes became my idols," Debs recalled. "Thomas Paine towered above them all. A thousand times . . . I have found inspiration and strength in the

A campaign poster for the fiery Socialist Party candidate Eugene V. Debs. (c. 1971–1972)

stirring words, 'These are the times that try men's souls.'" The First World War (1914–1918) tried Debs's soul. When he denounced the war and the government's persecution of war protesters, he was convicted of calling for rebellion and jailed. (President Harding commuted his ten-year sentence after Debs had served nearly three years.)[35]

Presidents have also turned to Paine for inspiration. Elected in 1828, Andrew Jackson was the first president to champion the "common man." A boy soldier during the War for Independence, he later rose to the rank of general. The seventh president had read *Rights of Man* as a youngster in frontier Tennessee. "Thomas Paine," Jackson wrote, "needs no monument by hands; he has erected a monument in the hearts of all who love liberty."[36]

None admired Paine more than the sixteenth president. Born in February 1809, four months before Paine died, Abraham Lincoln read *The Age of Reason* as a young man. His law partner, William Herndon, recalled that its ideas had such an impact that Lincoln "assimilated them into his own being."[37]

In line with Paine's work, Lincoln wrote a long essay criticizing organized religion, and especially Christianity. While he was reading the manuscript aloud, a friend grabbed it out of his hand and threw it into the fire. Friends feared that, if printed, it would ruin Lincoln's law practice and blast his ambitions for political office. Judge David Davis, an early backer, added: "He had no faith, in the Christian sense of the term." Yet, like Paine, Lincoln put his "faith in laws, principles, causes and effects." Ward Hill Lamon, a close friend, noted that "when he went to church at all, he went to mock, and came away to mimic." As Lincoln grew older, he became more cautious; not one mention of Paine or Deism appears in the complete edition of his writings and speeches. When he quoted from the Bible, it was not as a believer, but to drive home a point in a way he knew believers would understand.[38]

Lincoln modeled his speaking style on the Bible, the plays of William Shakespeare, and Thomas Paine's writings. Certain familiar phrases echo passages in *Common Sense* and *Rights of Man*. Like Paine, Lincoln believed in American exceptionalism. We remember that Paine called America "the last best hope of earth." Like Paine, too, Lincoln despised slavery. In 1858, he wrote: "As I would not be a *slave,* so I would not be a *master.* This is my idea of democracy. Whatever differs from this, to the extent of the difference, is not democracy." Finally, like Paine, he believed the United States could not exist without unity.[39]

On November 19, 1863, at the height of the Civil War, Lincoln gave the Gettysburg Address in memory of the Union soldiers killed in battle in Pennsylvania. Reading from a handwritten sheet of paper, the president voiced ideas straight out of *Rights of Man*. He said, "We here highly resolve that these dead shall not have died in vain—that this nation, under God, shall have a new birth of freedom—and that government of the people, by the people, for the people, shall not perish from the earth."[40]

President Franklin D. Roosevelt served in times as "interesting" as Lincoln's. In 1939, the German tyrant Adolf Hitler set out to conquer Europe. Meanwhile, on the other side of the globe, Japan aimed at dominating Asia. Only the U.S. Navy seemed able to upset its plans. To clear the way for conquest, on December 7, 1941, planes from Japanese aircraft carriers bombed the naval base at Pearl Harbor in the Hawaiian Islands. Hitler joined Japan, declaring war on the United States. The Second World War had begun.

Disasters followed like rapid drumbeats. Many Americans feared the war was already lost. Not Roo-

The Pearl Harbor Naval Base and the USS Shaw *ablaze after the attack by the Japanese. (December 7, 1941)*

sevelt. In peacetime, he had given "fireside chats," informal radio talks to explain his policies to the nation. On the evening of February 23, 1942, he spoke again from the White House. The president had a double task. First, he had to explain the military situation and the stakes involved. Second, he had to prepare the nation for the sacrifices that lay ahead.

Roosevelt linked past and present. The crisis we now face, he said, is really nothing new; democracy has *always* faced daunting challenges. After giving a detailed report of the fighting, he ended by recalling the winter of 1776, the darkest days of the War for Independence. "'These are the times that try men's souls,'" he read from the first pamphlet of Paine's *American Crisis*. Suddenly this and other phrases—"the summer soldier and the sunshine patriot," "tyranny, like hell, is not easily conquered"—took on fresh meaning.

"So spoke Americans in the year 1776. So speak Americans today!" Roosevelt concluded.[41]

Forty-three years later, President Ronald Reagan turned to *Common Sense* in another crisis. On November 20, 1985, he met with Soviet premier Mikhail Gorbachev in Geneva, Switzerland. The United States and the Soviet Union had been waging a "cold war" for four decades. Full of distrust and fear, they faced each other with millions of soldiers and thousands of atomic bombs capable of destroying life on earth.

President Reagan believed that he and the premier had a special responsibility, not only to their own countries but also to mankind. Human beings, he declared, were not wild beasts. If they used their God-given reason

The statue of Thomas Paine, carrying an inverted copy of his Rights of Man, *that stands in his hometown of Thetford, England. (c. March 2004)*

and showed some common sense, Americans and Soviets could settle their differences peacefully. "We have it in our power to start the world over again," he told Gorbachev.

"We have started something," Gorbachev replied. "To dialogue and cooperation!" From that day, the war clouds slowly began to part.[42]

Maybe somewhere the spirit of Thomas Paine was smiling.

Notes

Introduction: The Age of Paine

1. Thomas Clio Rickman, *Life of Thomas Paine* (London Thomas Clio Rickman, 1819), http://www.positiveatheism.org/hist/painric1.htm; Craig Nelson, *Thomas Paine: Enlightenment, Revolution, and the Birth of Modern Nations* (New York: Viking, 2006), 11; John Keane, *Tom Paine: A Political Life* (Boston: Little, Brown, 1995), 371; Paul Collins, *The Trouble with Tom: The Strange Afterlife and Times of Thomas Paine* (New York: Bloomsbury, 2005), 12.

2. Rickman, *Life of Thomas Paine;* Jack Fruchtman Jr., *Thomas Paine: Apostle of Freedom* (New York: Four Walls Eight Windows, 1994), 26; Vernon Louis Parrington, *Main Currents in American Thought,* 3 vols. (New York: Harcourt, Brace, 1930), 1:328.

3. Fruchtman, *Thomas Paine,* 101, 363, 398.

4. David Freeman Hawke, *Paine* (New York: Harper and Row, 1974), 2.

5. Keane, *Tom Paine,* xiii.

6. James Tepfer, "Thomas Paine: American Radical and Forerunner of the 21st Century," *Bulletin of Thomas Paine Friends* 9, no. 4 (Winter 2008–2009), http://www.thomas-paine-friends.org /tepfer-james_paine-as-american-radical.html.

1. Portrait of a Failure

1. Hawke, *Paine,* 8.

2. Roy Porter, *English Society in the Eighteenth Century* (New York: Penguin Books, 1990), 15; Gordon S. Wood, *The Radicalism of the American Revolution* (New York: Alfred A. Knopf, 1992), 27, 235.

3. Porter, *English Society,* 166.

4. Ibid., 18; Noel Rae, *The People's War: Original Voices of the American Revolution* (Guilford, CT: Lyons Press, 2012), 27.

5. Porter, *English Society*, 18.

6. Hawke, *Paine*, 10.

7. "18th Century London: Its Daily Life and Hazards," http://forums.canadiancontent.net/history/48176-18th-century-london-its-daily.html; Porter, *English Society*, 21.

8. Porter, *English Society*, 17.

9. Thomas Paine, *Collected Writings* (New York: Library of America, 1995), 633; Thomas Paine, *The Complete Writings of Thomas Paine*, ed. Philip S. Foner (New York: Citadel Press, 1945), 610, 617.

10. Rickman, *Life of Thomas Paine*.

11. Ibid.

12. Hawke, *Paine*, 11.

13. Keane, *Tom Paine*, 60.

14. Rickman, *Life of Thomas Paine*. Parliament consisted of branches, or "houses." The House of Lords included the hereditary representatives of the nobility and bishops of the Church of England. Elected representatives of the "commoners" served in the House of Commons, which controlled taxing and spending.

15. Thomas Paine, *Thomas Paine: Representative Selections*, ed. Harry Hayden Clark (New York: Hill and Wang, 1961), xci.

16. Keane, *Tom Paine*, 78; Hawke, *Paine*, 19, 21.

17. Hawke, *Paine*, 20.

18. Nelson, *Thomas Paine*, 13.

2. The Great American Cause

1. Thomas Paine, "African Slavery in America," http://www.constitution.org/tp/afri.htm.

2. Rae, *People's War*, 39–40.

3. Ibid., 41.

4. Henry Steele Commager and Richard B. Morris, eds., *The Spirit of 'Seventy-Six: The Story of the American Revolution as Told by Participants* (New York: Harper and Row, 1975), 3.

5. Jay Winik, *The Great Upheaval: America and the Birth of the Modern World, 1788–1800* (New York: HarperCollins, 2007), 77.

6. Harvey J. Kaye, *Thomas Paine: Firebrand of the Revolution* (New York: Oxford University Press, 2000), 16; Nelson, *Thomas Paine*, 76.

7. Paine, *Collected Writings*, 194.

8. Thomas Paine, *Common Sense*, ed. Isaac Kramnick (New York: Penguin Books, 1976), 63.

9. Ibid., 72.

10. Ibid., 77.

11. Ibid., 92.

12. Rae, *People's War*, 19, 23.

13. Ibid., 83.

14. Ibid., 84, 87, 111.

15. Ibid., 63, 82, 100, 120.

16. Keane, *Tom Paine*, 193.

17. Rickman, *Life of Thomas Paine.*

18. Keane, *Tom Paine*, 110.

19. Nelson, *Thomas Paine*, 93; Willard Sterne Randall, *Thomas Jefferson: A Life* (New York: Henry Holt, 1993), 260; Page Smith, *John Adams,* 2 vols. (Garden City, NY: Doubleday, 1962), 2:239–240.

20. Scott Liell, *46 Pages: Thomas Paine, "Common Sense," and the Turning Point to Independence* (Philadelphia: Running Press, 2003), 113; Nelson, *Thomas Paine*, 93.

21. Winik, *Great Upheaval,* 36, 156.

22. Catherine Drinker Bowen, *John Adams and the American Revolution* (Boston: Little, Brown, 1950), 604; Burke Davis, *Old Hickory: A Life of Andrew Jackson* (New York: Dial Press, 1977), 4; Winthrop D. Jordan, "Familial Politics: Thomas Paine and the Killing of the King, 1776," *Journal of American History* 60 (September 1973): 306–307; David McCullough, *1776* (New York: Simon and Schuster, 2005), 138.

23. Keane, *Tom Paine,* 141; David Hackett Fischer, *Washington's Crossing* (New York: Oxford University Press, 2004), 139.

24. Paine, *Collected Writings,* 91.

25. Nelson, *Thomas Paine,* 111.

26. Paine, *Collected Writings,* 101.

27. Keane, *Tom Paine,* 209.

28. Elkanah Watson, *Men and Times of the Revolution; or, Memoirs of Elkanah Watson* (New York: Dana, 1856), 108–109.

29. Paine, *Collected Writings,* 348.

30. Hawke, *Paine,* 137.

31. Fruchtman, *Thomas Paine,* 154.

32. Hawke, *Paine,* 163; Moncure D. Conway, *Thomas Paine,* 2 vols. (New York: Chelsea House, 1983), 2:280; John P. Kaminski, ed., *The Founders on the Founders: Word Portraits from the American Revolutionary Era* (Charlottesville: University of Virginia Press, 2008), 450.

33. Nelson, *Paine,* 49.

3. The Peculiar Honor of France

1. Keane, *Tom Paine,* 275.

2. Paine, *Complete Writings of Thomas Paine,* xxvii; Hawke, *Paine,* 190; Rickman, *Life of Thomas Paine.*

3. Winik, *Great Upheaval,* 108, 140; Christopher Hibbert, *The Days of the French Revolution* (New York: William Morrow, 1980), 19.

4. Ibid., 22, 26, 27.

5. Pierre de Beaumarchais, *"The Barber of Seville" and "The Marriage of Figaro,"* trans. John Wood (New York: Penguin Classics, 1964), 199–202. Wolfgang Amadeus Mozart later used an adaptation of the play as the libretto for his opera *The Marriage of Figaro.*

6. Simon Schama, *Citizens: A Chronicle of the French Revolution* (New York: Alfred A. Knopf, 1989), 420.

7. Winik, *Great Upheaval,* 120.

8. "Declaration of the Rights of Man," http://avalon.law.yale.edu/18th_century/rightsof.asp.

9. Porter, *English Society,* 349; William Wordsworth, "The French Revolution as It Appeared to Enthusiasts at Its Commencement."

10. Paine, *Complete Writings of Thomas Paine,* xxxii.

11. Fruchtman, *Thomas Paine,* 211.

12. Jean-Jacques Rousseau, *The Social Contract* (1762), book 1, section 1.

13. Edmund Burke, *Reflections on the Revolution in France,* Harvard Classics (New York: P. F. Collier and Son, 1909), 189, 226, 383.

14. Ibid., 244.

15. Ibid., 245.

16. Ibid., 227, 366.

17. Ibid., 368.

18. Paine, *Collected Writings,* 614.

19. Ibid., 436, 437, 453.

20. Ibid., 438.

21. Ibid., 479, 559.

22. Ibid., 582, 639.

23. Ibid., 540; Winik, *Great Upheaval,* 273.

24. Conway, *Thomas Paine,* 1:325.

25. "The Age of George III," http://www.historyhome.co.uk/c-eight/france/pitfrwar.htm; Porter, *English Society,* 350.

26. Hawke, *Paine,* 246, 248.

27. Paine, *Thomas Paine: Representative Selections,* ed. Clark, 369.

28. Hawke, *Paine,* 249; Nelson, *Thomas Paine,* 228; Conway, *Thomas Paine,* 2:29, 226.

29. Nelson, *Thomas Paine,* 232.

30. Paine, *Complete Writings of Thomas Paine,* xxxii.

31. E. P. Thompson, *The Making of the English Working Class* (New York: Vintage Books, 1966), 107.

32. Alfred Owen Aldridge, *Man of Reason: The Life of Thomas Paine* (Philadelphia: J. B. Lippincott, 1959), 78.

33. Winik, *Great Upheaval,* 303.

34. "Ça ira," http://en.wikipedia.org/wiki/%C3%87a_Ira.

35. Conway, *Thomas Paine,* 2:5.

36. Schama, *Citizens*, 621. France stopped using the guillotine in 1981, the year it abolished the death penalty.

37. Hibbert, *French Revolution*, 237.

38. Maximilien de Robespierre, "On the Moral and Political Principles of Domestic Policy" (speech, February 5, 1794), excerpted in "Justification of the Use of Terror," in *Modern History Sourcebook*, http://fordham.edu/halsall/mod/robespierre-terror.html.

39. Hibbert, *French Revolution*, 224, 225.

40. Fruchtman, *Thomas Paine*, 313; Nelson, *Thomas Paine*, 281; Keane, *Tom Paine*, 412.

41. Paine, *Complete Writings of Thomas Paine*, xxxv.

42. Keane, *Tom Paine*, 412.

43. Paine, *Thomas Paine: Representative Selections*, ed. Clark, 408.

44. Rickman, *Life of Thomas Paine*; Richard N. Rosenfeld, *American Aurora: A Democratic-Republican Returns: The Suppressed History of Our Nation's Beginnings and the Heroic Newspaper That Tried to Report It* (New York: St. Martin's Press, 1997), 33.

4. *The Age of Reason*

1. Theodore Roosevelt, *Gouverneur Morris* (New York: Charles Scribner's Sons, 1888), 289.

2. Keane, *Tom Paine*, 390; "John Adams on Thomas Paine's *Common Sense*, 1776," National Humanities Center Resource Toolbox, Making the Revolution: America, 1763–1791, http://www.nationalhumanitiescenter.org/pds/makingrev/rebellion/text7/adamscommonsense.pdf.

3. Michael Burleigh, *Earthly Powers: The Clash of Religion and Politics in Europe from the French Revolution to the Great War* (New York: HarperCollins, 2005), 100, 101.

4. Paine, *Representative Selections*, xx.

5. Adrienne Koch, ed., *The American Enlightenment: The Shaping of the American Experiment and a Free Society* (New York: George Braziller, 1965), 234; Nelson, *Thomas Paine*, 265.

6. Thomas Paine, "Of the Religion of Deism Compared with the Christian Religion," http://www.deism.com/paine_essay_deism_christianity.htm.

7. Benjamin Franklin, *Writings* (New York: Library of America, 1987), 1359; David L. Holmes, *The Faiths of the Founding Fathers* (New York: Oxford University Press, 2006), 54.

8. Paul F. Boller, *George Washington and Religion* (Dallas: Southern Methodist University Press, 1963), 82; Holmes, *Founding Fathers*, 69; Franklin Steiner, *The Religious Beliefs of Our Presidents: From Washington to F.D.R.* (Amherst, NY: Prometheus Books, 1995), 26–27.

9. Brooke Allen, "Our Godless Constitution," *Nation*, February 21, 2005, http://www.thenation.com/doc/20050221/allen/print?rel=opfollow.

10. Thomas Jefferson, *Writings* (New York: Library of America, 1983), 286; Holmes, *Founding Fathers*, 87.

11. Paine, *Collected Writings*, 666–667.

12. Ibid., 734, 747, 825, 827, 829.

13. Conway, *Thomas Paine*, 2:298.

14. Franklin, *Writings*, 748–749.

15. Porter, *English Society*, 165.

16. Nelson, *Thomas Paine*, 287, 299.

5. An Honest and Useful Life

1. Hawke, *Paine*, 143.

2. Harvey J. Kaye, *Thomas Paine and the Promise of America* (New York: Hill and Wang, 2005), 31.

3. Parrington, *Main Currents*, 1:312, 316.

4. Jefferson, *Writings*, 491.

5. Gordon S. Wood, *Empire of Liberty: A History of the Early Republic, 1789–1815* (New York: Oxford University Press, 2009), 178, 179; Jefferson, *Writings*, 1004.

6. Conway, *Thomas Paine*, 2:279.

7. Winik, *Great Upheaval*, 567–568; Edward J. Larson, *A Magnificent Catastrophe: The Tumultuous Election of 1800, America's First Presidential Campaign* (New York: Free Press, 2007), 169, 170; Holmes, *Founding Fathers*, 81; John Ferling, *Adams vs. Jefferson: The Tumultuous Election of 1800* (New York: Oxford University Press, 2004), 40, 154.

8. Michael Durey, "Thomas Paine's Apostles: Radical Émigrés and the Triumph of Jeffersonian Republicanism," *William and Mary Quarterly* 44, no. 4 (October 1987): 673–674.

9. Nelson, *Thomas Paine*, 267, 270.

10. Conway, *Thomas Paine*, 1:226; Wood, *Empire of Liberty*, 589.

11. Kaminski, *Founders on the Founders*, 458; Hawke, *Paine*, 294, 312, 354, 357.

12. Rosenfeld, *American Aurora*, 881; Nelson, *Thomas Paine*, 305; Winik, *Great Upheaval*, 579.

13. Keane, *Tom Paine*, 470, 471.

14. Nelson, *Thomas Paine*, 297; Hawke, *Paine*, 336.

15. Hawke, *Paine*, 382.

16. Wood, *Radicalism*, 327.

17. Ibid., 366.

18. George Washington, *Writings* (New York: Library of America, 1997), 1044.

19. Wood, *Radicalism*, 368.

20. Ferling, *Adams vs. Jefferson*, 213.

21. Keane, *Tom Paine*, 517.

22. Hawke, *Paine*, 390.

23. Conway, *Thomas Paine*, 1:vi.

24. Fruchtman, *Thomas Paine*, 433.

25. Nelson, *Thomas Paine*, 324.

26. Ibid.

27. Harry Harmer, *Tom Paine: The Life of a Revolutionary* (London: Haus Publishing, 2006), 106.

28. Porter, *English Society*, 350.

29. Ian Dyck, ed. *Citizen of the World: Essays on Thomas Paine* (London: Christopher Helm, 1987), 131.

30. Thompson, *English Working Class*, 498.

31. Fruchtman, *Thomas Paine*, 434; Leo A. Bressler, "Peter Porcupine and the Bones of Thomas Paine," *Pennsylvania Magazine of History and Biography*, April 1958, 184–185. See also Collins, *Trouble with Tom*.

32. Harmer, *Tom Paine*, 82.

33. Kaye, *Thomas Paine*, 128–129, 151–153.

34. Steven H. Jaffe, *Who Were the Founding Fathers? Two Hundred Years of Reinventing American History* (New York: Henry Holt, 1996), 51.

35. Ray Ginger, *The Bending Cross: A Biography of Eugene Victor Debs* (New Brunswick, NJ: Rutgers University Press, 1949), 25.

36. Kaye, *Thomas Paine*, 137.

37. William H. Herndon and Jesse W. Weik, *Abraham Lincoln: The True Story of a Great Life* (Scituate, MA: Digital Scanning, 2000), 439.

38. Ibid., 439–440; Ward Hill Lamon, *The Life of Abraham Lincoln: From His Birth to His Inauguration as President* (Lincoln: University of Nebraska Press, 1999), 486–487.

39. Abraham Lincoln, *The Collected Works of Abraham Lincoln*, ed. Roy P. Basler, 9 vols. (New Brunswick, NJ: Rutgers University Press, 1953–1955), 2:532, 5:537.

40. Ibid., 7:23.

41. Franklin D. Roosevelt, "Fireside Chat," February 23, 1942, http://www.presidency.ucsb.edu /ws/index.php?pid=16224.

42. Richard Reeves, *President Reagan: The Triumph of Imagination* (New York: Simon and Schuster, 2005), 293.

Image Credits

Arjayay: 15; **Louis-Léopold Boilly:** 88; **John Cassell:** 10; **George Cruikshank:** 108, 116; **Nathaniel Currier:** 37; **Jacques-Louis David:** 92; **Josef Hauzinger:** 67; **William Hogarth:** 18; **Homermeyn:** 144; **Library of Congress:** 2, 5, 9, 29, 30, 31, 34, 35, 38, 40, 41, 43, 48, 49, 50, 51, 52, 54, 55, 56, 59, 60, 62, 65, 69, 72, 77, 79, 82, 83, 86, 91, 93, 100, 103, 109, 120, 123, 126, 128, 138 (top), 139, 142; **John Seymour Lucas:** 19; **National Portrait Gallery:** 25; **New-York Historical Society:** 16, 132; **PD-US:** 3, 13, 20, 70, 75, 89, 95, 98, 107, 111, 135; **Shutterstock:** i, 7, 27, 63, 101, 117, 145; **United States Postal Service:** 138 (bottom)

Some More Things to Read

Books

Aldridge, Alfred Owen. *Man of Reason: The Life of Thomas Paine*. Philadelphia: J. B. Lippincott, 1959.

Bailyn, Bernard. *Faces of Revolution: Personalities and Themes in the Struggle for American Independence*. New York: Alfred A. Knopf, 1990.

Boller, Paul F. *George Washington and Religion*. Dallas: Southern Methodist University Press, 1963.

Burke, Edmund. *Reflections on the Revolution in France*. Harvard Classics, vol. 24, New York: P. F. Collier and Son, 1909.

Burleigh, Michael. *Earthly Powers: The Clash of Religion and Politics in Europe from the French Revolution to the Great War*. New York: HarperCollins, 2005.

Cobbett, William. *A Brief History of the Remains of the Late Thomas Paine, from the Time of Their Disinterment in 1819 by the Late William Cobbett, M.P., Down to the Year 1846*. London: J. Watson, 1847.

Collins, Paul. *The Trouble with Tom: The Strange Afterlife and Times of Thomas Paine*. New York: Bloomsbury, 2005.

Conway, Moncure D. *Thomas Paine*. 2 vols. New York: Chelsea House, 1983. First published in 1894, this is the first reliable biography of Paine.

Dyck, Ian, ed. *Citizen of the World: Essays on Thomas Paine*. London: Christopher Helm, 1987.

Ellis, Joseph J. *Passionate Sage: The Character and Legacy of John Adams*. New York: W. W. Norton, 2001.

Ferling, John. *Adams vs. Jefferson: The Tumultuous Election of 1800.* New York: Oxford University Press, 2004.

Fife, Graeme. *The Terror: The Shadow of the Guillotine: France, 1792–1794.* New York: St. Martin's Press, 2004.

Fischer, David Hackett. *Washington's Crossing.* New York: Oxford University Press, 2004.

Foner, Eric. *Tom Paine and Revolutionary America.* New York: Oxford University Press, 1976.

Fruchtman, Jack, Jr. *Thomas Paine: Apostle of Freedom.* New York: Four Walls Eight Windows, 1994.

Harmer, Harry. *Tom Paine: The Life of a Revolutionary.* London: Haus Publishing, 2006.

Hawke, David Freeman. *Paine.* New York: Harper and Row, 1974.

Herndon, William H., and Jesse W. Weik. *Abraham Lincoln: The True Story of a Great Life.* Scituate, MA: Digital Scanning, 2000.

Hibbert, Christopher. *The Days of the French Revolution.* New York: William Morrow, 1980.

Holmes, David L. *The Faiths of the Founding Fathers.* New York: Oxford University Press, 2006.

Jaffe, Steven H. *Who Were the Founding Fathers? Two Hundred Years of Reinventing American History.* New York: Henry Holt, 1996.

Jefferson, Thomas. *Writings.* New York: Library of America, 1983.

Kaminski, John P., ed. *The Founders on the Founders: Word Portraits from the American Revolutionary Era.* Charlottesville: University of Virginia Press, 2008.

Kaye, Harvey J. *Thomas Paine: Firebrand of the Revolution.* New York: Oxford University Press, 2000.

———. *Thomas Paine and the Promise of America.* New York: Hill and Wang, 2005.

Keane, John. *Tom Paine: A Political Life.* Boston: Little, Brown, 1995.

Lamon, Ward Hill. *The Life of Abraham Lincoln: From His Birth to His Inauguration as President.* Lincoln: University of Nebraska Press, 1999. Reprint of a book published in 1872.

Larson, Edward J. *A Magnificent Catastrophe: The Tumultuous Election of 1800, America's First Presidential Campaign.* New York: Free Press, 2007.

Liell, Scott. *46 Pages: Thomas Paine, "Common Sense," and the Turning Point to Independence.* Philadelphia: Running Press, 2003.

Maier, Pauline. *American Scripture: Making the Declaration of Independence.* New York: Alfred A. Knopf, 1997.

McCullough, David. *1776.* New York: Simon and Schuster, 2005.

Nelson, Craig. *Thomas Paine: Enlightenment, Revolution, and the Birth of Modern Nations.* New York: Viking, 2006.

Paine, Thomas. *Common Sense.* Edited by Isaac Kramnick. New York: Penguin Books, 1986.

———. *The Complete Writings of Thomas Paine.* Edited by Philip S. Foner. New York: Citadel Press, 1945.

———. *Paine: Political Writings.* Edited by Bruce Kuklick. Cambridge: Cambridge University Press, 1997.

———. *Thomas Paine: Collected Writings.* New York: Library of America, 1994.

———. *Thomas Paine: Representative Selections.* Edited by Harry Hayden Clark. New York: Hill and Wang, 1961.

Parrington, Vernon Louis. *Main Currents in American Thought.* 3 vols. New York: Harcourt, Brace, 1930.

Porter, Roy. *English Society in the Eighteenth Century.* New York: Penguin Books, 1990.

Powell, David. *Tom Paine: The Greatest Exile.* New York: St. Martin's Press, 1985.

Rae, Noel. *The People's War: Original Voices of the American Revolution.* Guilford, CT: Lyons Press, 2012.

Rickman, Thomas Clio. *The Life of Thomas Paine.* London: Thomas Clio Rickman, 1819, http://www.positiveatheism.org/hist/painric1.htm.

Rosenfeld, Richard N. *American Aurora: A Democratic-Republican Returns: The Suppressed History of Our Nation's Beginnings and the Heroic Newspaper That Tried to Report It.* New York: St. Martin's Press, 1997.

Scurr, Ruth. *Fatal Purity: Robespierre and the French Revolution.* New York: Henry Holt, 2006.

Steiner, Franklin. *The Religious Beliefs of Our Presidents: From Washington to F.D.R.* Amherst, NY: Prometheus Books, 1995.

Walters, Kerry S. *Benjamin Franklin and His Gods.* Urbana: University of Illinois Press, 1999.

Winik, Jay. *The Great Upheaval: America and the Birth of the Modern World, 1788–1800.* New York: HarperCollins, 2007.

Wood, Gordon S. *Empire of Liberty: A History of the Early Republic, 1789–1815.* New York: Oxford University Press, 2009.

———. *The Radicalism of the American Revolution*. New York: Alfred A. Knopf, 1992.

Articles

Allen, Brooke. "Our Godless Constitution." *Nation,* February 21, 2005. http://www.thenation.com/doc/20050221/allen/print?rel=opfollow.

Barry, Alyce. "Thomas Paine: Privateersman." *Pennsylvania Magazine of History and Biography,* October 1977, 451–461.

Bressler, Leo A. "Peter Porcupine and the Bones of Thomas Paine." *Pennsylvania Magazine of History and Biography,* April 1958, 176–185.

Durey, Michael. "Thomas Paine's Apostles: Radical Émigrés and the Triumph of Jeffersonian Republicanism." *William and Mary Quarterly* 44, no. 4 (October 1987): 662–688.

Tepfer, James. "Thomas Paine: American Radical and Forerunner of the 21st Century." *Bulletin of Thomas Paine Friends,* Winter 2008–2009. http://www.thomas-paine-friends.org/tepfer-james_paine-as-american-radical.html.

Walvin, James A. "The English Jacobins, 1789–1799." *Historical Reflections/ Réflexions Historiques* 4, no. 1 (Summer 1977): 91–109. http://www.jstor.org/stable/41290693.

Wecter, Dixon. "Thomas Paine and the Franklins." *American Literature* 12, no. 3 (November 1940): 306–331.

Internet Sources

Liberty Online Thomas Paine Library
libertyonline.hypermall.com/Paine/Default.htm

Thomas Paine National Historical Association
thomaspaine.org

Thomas Paine Society UK
thomaspaineuk.com

Additional information about Thomas Paine
bbc.co.uk/history/british/empire_seapower/paine_01.shtml

Index

Note: *Italic* page numbers refer to illustrations.

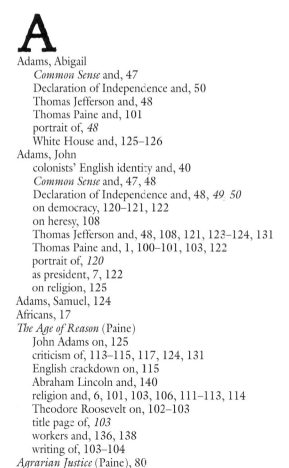

I

ideas
  American Revolution as crusade for, 44–45
  power of, 21–22
  role in society, 4
immigrants, 124
independence; *see also* Declaration of Independence
  colonists' English identity and, 39–40
  Common Sense and, 42, 44
Industrial Revolution, 134
Intolerable Acts, 36–37
Islam, 107

J

Jackson, Andrew, 50, 140
James II (king of England), 11
Japan, 142
Jefferson, Thomas
  John Adams and, 48, 108, 121, 123–124, 131
  colonists' English identity and, 39
  Common Sense and, 47, 48
  Declaration of Independence and, 48, *49, 50*
  on democracy, 130–131
  French Revolution and, 122
  limits on federal power and, 121–122
  Louisiana Purchase and, 127
  on Louis XVI, 66
  Thomas Paine and, 62–63, 65, 117, 125, 127, 133
  portrait of, *123*
  as president, 7, 123–124
  religious freedom and, 110–111
Jews, 68, 108
jihads, 107
John (king of England), *10,* 11
Johnson, Samuel, 12
Joseph II (emperor of Austria), 67
Judaism, 112
Julius Caesar, 121

K

Kearsley, John, 29
King of Prussia (privateer), 20–21

L

Lafayette, Marquis de, 71
Lambert, Mary, 22
Lamon, Ward Hill, 141
Laurens, John, 57–58
left wing, 92
Lewis, Meriwether, 127
Lexington, Massachusetts, 37, 40, 43
liberty; *see also* Sons of Liberty
  civil liberties, 118–119
  Common Sense and, 46, 80
  French Revolution and, 71, 93, 95, 122
  as theme in Thomas Paine's writing, 6, 7, 113
The Life and Morals of Jesus of Nazareth (The Jefferson
    Bible), 111, *111*
Lincoln, Abraham, 4, 45, 140–141
Livingston, Robert, 48
London, England, 17–20, *18*
London Corresponding Society, *81*
London Packet (ship), 26, 27, 28–29
Louisiana Purchase, 127
Louis XVI (king of France)
  absolute power of, 66–67
  execution of, 90–91, *91,* 92
  French and Indian War and, 57
  French Revolution and, 69–70, 89–90
  portrait of, *67*

M

Madison, James, 7, 60, *60,* 108
Magna Carta, *10, 11, 108*
Mao Zedong, 94
Marie Antoinette (queen of France), 67, *67,* 91, *92*
The Marriage of Figaro (Beaumarchais), 68–69
Martin, Benjamin, 21
mathematics, 21–22, 109
Maximilian Franz, Archduke of Austria, *67*
Menzies, Edward, 20
Middle East, 107
Mississippi River, 127
moderates, 92
monarchy
  Common Sense and, 42
  Thomas Paine on, 90
  revolutions and, 72
  right to govern and, 5
  wealth and, 11–12
Monroe, James, 7, 97–98, 99, *100,* 104
Morris, Gouverneur, 96, 97, 102–103
Mott, Lucretia, 137
Muslims, 107

N

Napoleon Bonaparte, 77, *77*, 97, 116, 117, 127, 131
Napoleonic Wars, 116
natural rights
    Edmund Burke on, 75–76
    Declaration of Independence and, 49
    Declaration of the Rights of Man and the Citizen, 70–71
    Enlightenment and, 73
    Rights of Man and, 6, 78–79
New Orleans, Louisiana, 127
New Rochelle, New York, 61, 128, *128*, 133
Newton, Isaac, 21–22, *25*, 108–109, *109*
Newtonians, 21–22
Notes on the State of Virginia (Jefferson), 111

O

Ollive, Elizabeth, 23, 24–25
Ottawa Indians, 16

P

Pain, Frances, 8–9, 10, 65
Pain, Joseph, 8–10, 14–15, 16, 65
Paine, Thomas; *see also The Age of Reason* (Paine); *The American Crisis* (Paine); *Common Sense* (Paine); *Rights of Man* (Paine)
    alcohol and, 128–129
    American Revolution and, 6–7, 40–41, 52–55, 57–59, 71, 86, 124, 143
    appearance of, 1–2
    boyhood and youth of, 8–10, *9*, 11, 14–22
    bridge design of, 61–63, *62*, 65
    burial of, 132–133, 136
    business failures of, 22–26
    death of, 132
    on Deism, 109–110
    as editor, 30–32
    education of, 4, 14–15, 21
    as Enlightenment intellectual, 4–6, 42
    as exciseman, 22–24, 25, 33, 85
    finances of, 60–61
    French Revolution and, 3, 6–7, 71–73, 76, 78–81, 85–86, 89, 95–99, 104, 106, 115–116
    Greenwich Village house of, 131–132, *132*
    immigration to America, 26, 27, 28–29
    Thomas Jefferson and, 62–63, 65, 117, 125, 127, 133
    legacy of, 137–144
    marriage to Mary Lambert, 22
    marriage to Elizabeth Ollive, 23, 24–25
    mission to seek French aid, 57–58, 59
    New Rochelle property of, 61, 128, *128*, 133
    old age of, 128–133
    papers of, 3
    personality of, 2–3, 58
    political cartoons of, *79, 81, 83, 86,* 115, *116*
    portraits of, *2, 5*
    postage stamp, *138*
    scientific interests of, 21, 61–63
    signature of, *3*
    on slavery, 30–32
    statue of, 137, *144*
    stroke of, 131
    George Washington and, 6–7, 53, 60–61, 84, 99–100, 124
    will of, 132
pamphlets, 40–41
Pearl Harbor Naval Base, 142, *142*
Pennsylvania Magazine, 30
Pennsylvania Volunteers, 52
Philadelphia, Pennsylvania, 29–31, *29*
Pitt, William, 82–83
poverty
    equality before the law and, 11–14
    London life and, 17–20, *18*
    Thomas Paine's fear of, 60
    Thomas Paine's sympathy for the poor, 3, 19–20, 47
    Philadelphia and, 29
    riots in England and, 18–19, *19*
printing press, *30*
privateers, 16–17, *16*, 20–21
property ownership, 11–13, 23
Protestants, 10, 68, 107–108, 113

Q

Quakers, 9–10, 14–15

R

Reagan, Ronald, 143–144
reason, 22, 109–110
Reflections on the Revolution in France (Burke), 74–78, *75*
religion
    The Age of Reason and, 6, 101, 103, 106, 111–113, 114
    Bill of Rights and, 119
    in France, 68, 74, 89, 104–105
    history of conflicts, 106–108
    Thomas Jefferson on, 110–111

V

Vietnam War, 46

W

War for Independence, *see* American Revolution
Washington, George
    John Adams and, 122
    colonists' English identity and, 39–40
    Common Sense and, 47
    Deism and, 10
    French Revolution and, 71
    Alexander Hamilton and, 73
    Thomas Paine and, 6–7, 53, 60–61, 84, 99–100, 124
    on political parties, 130
    as president, 6–7, 69
    as Revolutionary War general, 38–39, *38*, 52–54, 56–58, *56*, *59*
    Rights of Man dedicated to, 78
Washington, D.C., 126–127, 138
Watson, Elkanah, 58
White House, 125–126, *126*, 143
Wilson, Bird, 110
women
    executions and, 13–14, *13*
    rights of, 11–12, 137–138
Wordsworth, William, 71
Wright, Fanny, 137, *138*

Y

Yorktown, Virginia, 58, *59*